The Complete Guide to this Disorder

by Bill Habets

TINNITUS

Published in Great Britain MCMXCV *by Carnell plc,*
28 Eccleston Square, London SW1V 1PU

Typeset by Typesetting Solutions, Slough, Berks.

Printed by Repro City Limited, London.

ISBN 1-85779-755-8

Table of Contents

Foreword

Tinnitus is a very common disorder affecting something like about one in ten of all adults. Despite this high rate of prevalence, only comparatively little research is currently being funded into finding out how tinnitus can be alleviated. Part of the reason for this are the severe budget restrictions affecting the National Health Service as a whole; another reason, generally left unstated, is that there are currently few avenues left open to scientific investigation that are likely to yield major results in the very near future. Nevertheless, research does go on and while no one is predicting any dramatic breakthrough soon, there is a steady accumulation of greater understanding of what causes tinnitus, how it may be prevented, and – perhaps most importantly – how its symptoms can be alleviated by a wide range of therapies.

In the meantime, a tinnitus sufferer, after having gone through the whole gamut of what the professionals can offer, is eventually faced with the conclusion that their condition remains uncured and essentially unchanged. That, however, does not mean that there is not a great deal that can be done to minimise both the symptoms of tinnitus and their impact, just that this help will not necessarily be coming from the expected medical sources, but rather from other approaches, these including many simple 'self-help' techniques.

As many a tinnitus sufferer will gladly testify, planning and executing your own self-help programme is often an excellent way to bring tinnitus under control. Naturally, it is important that before you embark on this course you should first have all the medical tests and investigations necessary to exclude the possibility that your tinnitus is caused by some other underlying disorder, or that it can indeed be cured by medical intervention.

Because what you can do yourself to reduce your tinnitus – or the extent it affects you – is so often the key to making the disorder fade into lesser significance, a large part of this book has been devoted to providing recommendations and suggestions for self-help techniques that have helped many others in the past, and it is my hope that these can also help you.

However, as you read on, please bear two most important points in mind:

Firstly, a book like this one cannot be – nor is it intended to be – in any way a substitute for professional medical advice. Readers are, therefore, earnestly urged to always consult their own doctor before trying out any kind of therapy not prescribed by medically-qualified professionals, starting a new diet, or engaging in what for them is a new form of physical exercise. Only your own doctor – or consultant – can help you decide what may or may not be helpful or appropriate in the specific circumstances of your own case.

Secondly, although the information offered in this book is based upon the views of doctors, specialists and other health professionals, these experts are by no means always in total agreement about many aspects of tinnitus. This means that there are dissenting opinions in many areas, and whenever this is the case I've tried to provide a balanced view of all sides of a particular argument.

Finally, I'd like to say a 'thank you' to all those who have given so generously of their time and expertise during my research. While they are too many to mention individually, to each and every one of them, my sincere and appreciative thanks.

Bill Habets

CHAPTER 1

What is Tinnitus?

It's not all that easy to come up with a totally satisfactory definition of tinnitus because almost invariably there will be exceptions to almost anything you might state categorically to describe it. To illustrate this point, there is even some dispute and confusion about whether 'tinnitus' is a disorder in its own right or merely a label that conveniently identifies a number of broadly similar symptoms.

For example, the authors of one standard medical dictionary plainly saw tinnitus primarily as a symptom when they defined it as 'any noise (buzzing, ringing, etc.) in the ear'. That definition is fine as far as it goes, but totally ignores the fact that for many sufferers tinnitus is seen as a disorder or a condition of some sort that is the cause of their symptoms.

It follows from this that the word tinnitus, depending upon the context within which it is used, can have a curious dual meaning, so at times possibly denoting two quite different things:

1) Tinnitus can simply mean, as suggested by the dictionary quoted above, 'a noise heard in the ear', or

2) The word can describe a disorder of hearing whose main symptom is that the sufferer experiences sounds for which there is no matching source in the environment. But, as we shall see later, this already broad definition still isn't quite wide enough because it doesn't include that form of tinnitus in which the sufferer hears non-environmental sounds that in fact have origins in his or her own body. What's more, *this* definition also fails to include those situations where the

> tinnitus noises are doubtlessly the symptoms of some other clearly defined disorder. It also needs to be pointed out that the noises of tinnitus are by no means always heard in the ear; many sufferers describe their symptoms as 'sensing noises' somewhere in their head.

While it would be useful if there were one word to denote tinnitus as a symptom and another to indicate it as a disorder, this unfortunately isn't the case. This means that throughout this book the word tinnitus will of necessity have been used as it has been traditionally, to either denote the symptom of noises heard in the ear or, in its broader sense, as a general label for a disorder or, if you prefer, an ailment or complaint.

Incidentally, for most people affected by tinnitus, there is little doubt as to exactly what the word means to them: it's the disorder, condition, ailment, call it what you like, that afflicts them, and the symptoms this produces usually are simply described by them as 'noises' rather than tinnitus.

A Very Ancient Problem

The term tinnitus is derived from the Latin word *tinnire*, this meaning a ringing or tinkling sound.

Because many forms of tinnitus are the result of overexposure to very loud high noise levels over lengthy periods, it is assumed by some that the complaint is a malady of modern times and perhaps didn't exist in earlier days when life was allegedly simpler and probably less noisy. It's a nice theory, but one that's not borne out by the facts, as references to tinnitus are to be found in the earliest medical writings dating back to the dawning of civilisation in early Mesopotamia and Egypt. In more recent times, tinnitus is frequently mentioned in the medical literature of the day, suggesting that it was just as common a complaint then as it is now.

It is hard to say whether tinnitus is on the increase, although there is plenty of evidence to suggest that there are more recorded cases of it nowadays than ever before, this leaving open the question as to just how many instances of tinnitus might have gone unrecorded in the recent past. Most experts, however, agree that it is likely that more people than ever before have tinnitus today, or are at greater risk of eventually developing it, this increase being brought about by several quite different factors, including:

- Many cases of tinnitus can be traced back to previous exposure to sounds that were loud enough to cause hearing loss, this loss usually taking place almost imperceptibly over many years, if not decades. While modern technology has brought us the benefits of an endless variety of home entertainment in the form of television, tapes, records and videos, it has also enabled us to listen to these at volume levels high enough to ultimately damage hearing. What's more, for many, listening to very loud music is not just an occasional pastime, but something they choose to be exposed to for many hours every day, as exemplified by the popularity of the ubiquitous Walkman and similar devices.

- There is little doubt that, mainly because of increased road traffic, our towns and cities have generally become noisier places, the cumulative effect of this noise pollution taking a toll on the hearing of the inhabitants. There is also some evidence to suggest that tinnitus stemming from working or having previously worked in noisy environments may be on the increase, despite various regulations meant to control noise levels in the workplace.

- Even medical advances in other fields may have contributed to increasing the risk of tinnitus. Several drugs used to treat quite ordinary conditions have been found to be able to trigger the problem in susceptible people.

- Another reason why a larger percentage of the population may nowadays have tinnitus is because, on the average, we live longer than our ancestors. A very common form of tinnitus is the one that is associated with a kind of hearing loss that occurs mainly as part of the ageing process. As more people live longer, greater numbers reach the age when tinnitus is likely to become noticeable.

Incidence and Prevalence

When considering how widespread tinnitus is, there are two separate aspects to be taken into account: its *prevalence* and *incidence*, two words that are sometimes carelessly used as meaning the same thing, but which have quite different definitions:

- Prevalence – also known as the *prevalence rate* – is a measurement based on the number of people affected by the condition in a given population.

- Incidence – also known as the *incidence rate* or *inception rate* – is a measurement, usually obtained by statistical methods, of the number of *new* episodes of an illness or disorder arising in a given population over a specific period of time. Incidence is most often expressed as 'so many people affected' or 'episodes of the disorder per 1000 individuals at risk'. In tinnitus, of course, there will almost invariably only be one episode per individual affected, unlike other ailments, such as influenza which someone may have more than once within the time period being studied.

While there is unanimous agreement amongst experts that tinnitus is extremely common, there is, however, some discrepancy between the statistics from various sources, but the following figures are generally accepted as reflecting most accurately the magnitude of the problem:

- The British Tinnitus Association says that 'more than four million British adults have tinnitus, as do a large number of children, almost certainly from birth'. While no exact figures are available for the number of children affected, one estimate extrapolated from other statistics puts this as high as possibly a million.

- A fairly old study – but one that provides an interesting point of reference – is the one carried out by random sampling between 1957 and 1959. It found that nearly 40 per cent of those older than 55 years had a history of tinnitus, as did more than 20 per cent of people aged between 18 and 24. However, these very high figures need to be discounted somewhat because they also include instances where the tinnitus lasted only a very short time and didn't recur thereafter.

- A more recent research project, also based on random sampling, by the Institute of Hearing led to the following suggestion: that a more realistic prevalence figure was 17 per cent of the UK population, this including only those cases where the symptoms were constant or present most of the time, and excluding those where the noises were only heard temporarily. Incidentally, the same study also found that people in manual occupations were twice as likely to have tinnitus than those doing non-manual work.

Even more revealing of the massive effect that tinnitus has on the everyday lives of people afflicted by it are figures showing *how much* it affects them. In a recently published document, the British Tinnitus Association said that of the four million plus sufferers in the United Kingdom:

- More than 200,000 of them experienced symptoms so severe that they were unable to lead a normal life.

- About 437,000 were afflicted to the extent that they described the quality of their life as being 'severely affected'.

- More than 655,000 said that they were 'severely annoyed' by their tinnitus.

- Nearly 1.1 million described their tinnitus as 'moderately annoying'.

The sufferers falling into the four categories above add up to about 2.5 million, leaving some 1.5 million adult sufferers whose symptoms are causing relatively little discomfort, annoyance or interference with daily life.

While statistics are always open to some interpretation or liable to slight error, there is little doubt that tinnitus is a health problem of massive proportions, affecting perhaps as many as one in ten of the population at one time or another. To make matters worse, tinnitus is all too often a medically incurable condition, with most sufferers having to find a way to live with it, as confirmed by this comment from the British Tinnitus Association: 'For the great majority of sufferers, the most they can hope for is relief from the consequences of tinnitus . . . Proper counselling can also teach people to adjust to the condition. But personal management of it has to be learned, often with difficulty and most hospitals are poorly equipped to teach these techniques.'

That last quote may appear to suggest a bleak outlook for most tinnitus sufferers, but in fact that isn't necessarily the case. Hundreds of thousands of sufferers – some of them with very severe tinnitus – have found ways of overcoming or minimising their problem, using methods and techniques like those described in later chapters of this book.

CHAPTER 2

How Hearing Works

To fully understand the various things that can go wrong with our hearing – including, of course, the possible development of tinnitus – it's useful to first of all understand how human hearing works. Incidentally, it's worth noting that the original function of the ear in creatures lower down the evolutionary ladder wasn't to perceive sounds but instead to control the proper positioning of the body in three-dimensional space. In fact, the maintaining of balance is still the ear's principal function – even its only function – in many species.

In humans, hearing – which can be roughly defined as the receiving and interpreting of sounds – is an extremely complex process, involving many different aspects. Although the ears are generally viewed as the organs of hearing, the correct recognition of sounds also requires the proper functioning of the auditory pathway – a series of stages through which nerve impulses are eventually transmitted to the brain.

However, to begin at the beginning, let us start by looking at the ear, which in all higher verterbrates (but also in some more primitive animals) consists of three main parts:

1) The outer ear (also known as the *external* ear). This consists not only of what is commonly called the ear (the flap of skin and cartilage on the side of the head), but also includes the tube that leads from the ear to the eardrum.

2) The middle ear (also known as the *tympanum* or tympanic cavity). This is an irregularly shaped, air-filled

cavity located beyond the eardrum where the vibrations received by the eardrum are then transmitted via a series of small bones to the oval window which lies at the start of the inner ear.

3) The inner ear (also known as the internal ear or sometimes referred to as the *labyrinth*). As suggested by the latter of these names, this part of the ear is made up of a convoluted system of cavities and ducts, most of which are concerned with maintaining balance, but also a large central cavity – the *cochlea* – where the received sound impulses are processed and transformed into signals that stimulate the nerves of hearing.

Let us now look at these various parts in greater detail:

The Outer Ear

There are two parts to the outer ear: the *auricle* or *pinna* (that is the visible part which lies outside the head and which is that part of the body most commonly understood as being described by the word 'ear' when used generally); and the *external auditory meatus*, a tube that leads through the temporal bone of the skull to the eardrum.

The auricle serves but little – if any – auditory purpose in man as it's too small to make a great contribution to the efficiency of the collection of sound. Neither can the human auricle be moved to an extent sufficient to help pinpoint where a sound may be originating. While the human ear can be slightly moved through the action of three muscles (the *anterior, superior* and *posterior auricular* muscles), most people are unaware of this possibility, although a few have developed the ability of move their ears, this feat, however, usually being a party trick rather than an way of heightening hearing.

In contrast to man, many animals – especially those with larger or funnel-shaped auricles – can exert considerable muscular force on their auricles and so considerably improve their ability to collect sounds. Incidentally, there is little doubt that man – or his Darwinian ancestors – once had greater conscious muscular control of his ears and used this as part of his survival skills. In many ways, it's a great shame that this ability was more or less lost as we climbed the evolutionary ladder, because even now you can easily test how greatly a mobile ear can heighten sound awareness by gently manipulating the shape of your ears so that they are directed at what would otherwise be a faint sound source.

Inside the auricle lies a hollow - called the *concha* - and it is in the deepest part of this that the external auditory meatus begins. This meatus - in anatomy, the word means a passage or opening - is usually about an inch long and slightly curved in shape, with approximately the first third of it being cartilaginous and the remaining two thirds being bony.

The external auditory meatus is lined throughout by skin, which contains both sebaceous and ceruminous glands, the latter being believed to be sweat glands that are modified so that instead of secreting sweat they produce *cerumen*, the medical name given to earwax. An excessive production and/or accumulation of earwax can, of course, be responsible for both deafness and tinnitus, something that will be dealt with in greater detail in Chapter 5.

The Middle Ear

At the innermost end of the outer ear's external auditory canal lies the eardrum, which consists of a membrane made of skin and collagen fibres that, unless damaged, completely seals off the outer ear from the middle ear. A muscle - the *tensor tympani* - that runs from the eardrum to the wall of the middle ear keeps the eardrum under tension, so making it more responsive to sound waves.

A chain of very small bones - called the *auditory ossicles* - are located in the middle ear and their job is to transmit and magnify the vibrations perceived by the eardrum to the oval window which lies at the opposite end of the middle ear. There are three ossicles, the first two acting as levers upon the next one in the chain and the last one acting directly upon the opening to the inner ear:

- ♦ The first ossicle is the hammer (the *malleus*) and it is attached to the upper part of the eardrum and therefore responds to vibrations induced there by sound waves, transmitting and amplifying these to the next ossicle.

- In the middle of the chain of ossicles is the anvil (the *incus*). This receives vibrations from the hammer, and amplifies these once more, before transmitting them further along the line.

- Last in line is the stirrup (the *stapes*), its non-medical name stemming from its shape which does indeed resemble that of a stirrup. The innermost end of the stirrup lies directly upon the oval window, the small opening in the skull that marks the entrance to the inner ear. The stirrup receives vibrations from the anvil and amplifies these as it transmits them to the oval window.

As you can see, the ossicles provide three separate stages at which the sound vibrations are magnified, the amount of amplification becoming greater and greater as the vibrations proceed along the chain.

However, apart from that produced by the lever effect of the ossicles, further amplification takes place within the middle ear because vibrations captured by the eardrum – which has a relatively large surface, this averaging 85 square millimeters – are eventually received by the oval window whose average surface is only 3.2 square millimeters. This difference in surface areas creates amplification because when the same amount of force is applied to a smaller surface, its intensity is increased, and this is exactly what happens with the pressure created by sound. One way of understanding this effect is by thinking of a given amount of rain falling down. If all of the rain is spread over a large surface – like a lawn – then each square foot of it will only receive a small amount. However, should all of the same quantity of rain be concentrated within a single square foot, that area would indeed be subjected to a veritable deluge.

The two amplification processes in the middle ear – that of the lever action of the ossicles plus that resulting from the different sizes of the surfaces of the eardrum and the oval window – combine to bring about a massive total amount of amplification, the vibrations reaching the inner ear being between 20 and 25 times more powerful than they were when received by the eardrum. Because the effect of this magnification can, in fact, be too intense when the sound level is extremely high, there is also a mechanism through which it can be automatically damped down, and this consists of a muscle – the *stapedial* muscle – that reduces the build up of oscillations in the ossicles by pulling the stirrup somewhat away from the oval window. Unfortunately, this damping down effect depends on reflex action, and this reacts too slowly to allow people to avoid the damage that may be caused by very sudden and extremely loud noises, such as gunfire.

Other Aspects of the Middle Ear

As has been noted briefly, the middle ear – like the outer ear – is an air-filled cavity. Naturally, so that the eardrum responds only to air pressure caused by sound waves, it is vital that the air pressure within both the inner and outer ears be the same. Should the pressures not be equal, the eardrum would become artificially distended inward or outward, depending upon whether the air pressure in the middle ear was higher or lower than that created by atmospheric pressure in the outer ear. This equalisation of pressure is achieved through very narrow conduits – the *Eustachian tubes* – one which connects each inner ear to the *pharynx*, that being the tube that extends to the top of the oesophagus to the base of the skull, and links into the mouth and the nasal cavity. Most of the time, the Eustachian tubes are closed, but they open – in response to involuntary muscular action – when you swallow or yawn. If the pressure in the middle ear at that moment is not identical to atmospheric pressure, then either more air will be admitted to, or some will released from, the middle ear through these tubes.

Incidentally, it is to open these tubes that you're often advised to swallow when you're gaining height rapidly in an aircraft, a time when the atmospheric pressure may be changing quickly depending upon how effective the plane's pressurisation is. Swallowing at that time will often be marked by a brief 'popping' noise in the ears, this being the result the eardrum responding to air pressure equalisation in the middle ear.

Of course, it would seem that the whole problem of matching the air pressure in the middle ear to that of atmospheric pressure would never have arisen had Mother Nature chosen to design the Eustachian tubes so that they were permanently open. There is, however, a very good reason why the tubes are closed most of the time, as this reduces the risk of infection affecting the middle ear. This natural fail-safe mechanism can nevertheless be defeated when you blow your nose too violently, as this can drive infected material through the Eustachian tubes into the middle ear, possibly resulting in earache or temporarily diminished hearing.

It also needs to be noted that the middle ear provides another important function as it transforms the sound vibrations captured by the eardrum – which, of course, are vibrations occuring in air – into vibrations which are better suited for being transmitted in fluid, the inner ear lying at the other side of the oval window being a fluid-filled cavity. Fluid offers a different type of resistance to the transmission of vibrations than air, and this is also one of the reasons why the signals received by the eardrum have to be amplified before they reach the inner ear.

The Inner Ear

On the other side of the oval window lies the inner ear. It is filled with a special fluid called *perilymph* and contains a number of cavities, most of which are concerned with balance (about which more later), but also one – the *cochlea* – where the sound vibrations are transformed into impulses which can travel along the nerves to the brain.

The cochlea is a tube within which lie three more tubes. Overall, the cochlea is spiral-shaped, looking rather like a sea shell or about two and a half turns of a slightly unwound clock spring. The widest part of the cochlea lies near and just below the oval window. Just below that, the cochlea is also linked to another window – the round window – that lies between the middle and the inner ear.

The three tubes within the cochlea are:

1) The *scala vestibuli,* also called the *vestibular canal*. This is open to the perilymph of the inner ear.

2) The *scala tympani,* also called the *tympanic canal.* This tube also contains perilymph, and links to the round window. The scala vestibuli and the scala tympani are in fact connected by a very small opening – the helicotrema – at the very end of the cochlea, but the size of this opening is so minute that it greatly restricts the amount of perilymph that can flow through it.

3) Sandwiched between these two tubes is the third one, the *cochlear duct* (also called the *scala media*), which is filled with a different fluid – the *endolymph* – and which contains the *organ of Corti* (also known as the *spiral organ*), a very complex structure that converts sound signals into nerve impulses that are then transmitted via the cochlear nerve to the brain.

The ochlea marks an important stage in the process of hearing because it is here that sounds that hitherto had been vibrations, transmitted through the air, via resonating bones or membranes, or through fluid, are metamorphosed into nerve impulses that can be sent to and recognised by the brain.

Broadly speaking, this is how the sounds are changed from one form into the other:

- Vibrations resulting from the action of the stapes on the oval window are transmitted via the perilymph to the scala vestibuli of the cochlea.

- The vibrations affect the pressure in both the scala vestibuli and the scala tympani. Naturally, these changes in pressure also affect the cochlear duct as it lies between the other two scalas.

- As already mentioned, within the cochlear duct is the organ of Corti and this, in part, consists of a continuous membrane – the *basilar membrane* – whithin which are embedded some 30,000 sensory cells from which protrude very thin hairs. The upper ends of these hairs are embedded in another membrane, the *tectorial membrane.*

- As the cochlear duct becomes distorted in response to altering pressures in the surrounding scalas, this distortion also affects the tectorial membrane, causing it to exert a tugging action on the hair cells. The stimulus created by this pulling action then triggers the hair cells into setting off nervous impulses which are then transmitted by nerve fibres to eventually reach the brain.

Maintaining Balance

As already mentioned earlier, the inner ear also contains other cavities whose correct functioning, although not directly connected with hearing, can also become affected when there is inner ear infection. In certain instances, hearing problems will also be accompanied by disturbances in the sense of balance – this combination of symptoms, of course, being a pointer suggesting that the origin of disorder is likely to be somewhere in the inner ear. For that reason, it is worth taking a brief look at these other organs, which include:

- Three semi-circular canals – one of which lies more or less horizontally, and two of which are vertical with their planes at 90 degrees to each other. Between them, these three structures can be said to represent two adjoining sides and the floor of a cube. Each of these canals is about 15mm long and lies within ducts in the bone of the skull. At the end of each canal lies a somewhat wider area – the *ampulla* – that contains sensory cells which detect movements in the fluid within the canals and then translate this information into nervous impulses.

- The *utriculus* – also called the *utricle* – is an endolymph-filled membranous sac that contains a sensory macula that lies more or less horizontally, and whose hairs respond to gravity and translate this data into nervous impulses that are sent to the brain, providing the latter with information about how the head is currently positioned.

- Similar to but much smaller than the utriculus is the *sacculus* - also known as the *saccule* - which also contains a sensory macula, but one that is positioned more or less vertically, that also responds to gravity and provides the brain with information about the position of the head. There is, however, some doubt about the exact role of the sacculus in humans, some experts believing that it may not be greatly involved in controlling balance, but may instead be partly involved in hearing, especially in the recognition of sounds of very low frequencies.

This is how the five separate, but cross-linked, organs work in harmony to control both body balance and posture:

- The three semi-circular canals - acting together somewhat like a trio of builders' levels - provide the brain with information to maintain the body's overall balance by setting off reflex actions in various muscles to place the body in its currently desired position.

- On the other hand the utriculus - aided to some extent by the sacculus - provides the brain with the information it needs to maintain posture.

Naturally, the brain also receives information about balance and posture from other sources, notably from the eyes and feedbaack from various muscles, and all of this additional data is amalgamated with that coming from the inner ear cavities. Dizziness, poor balance, deficient co-ordination are all problems that can arise when there is a discord between the information coming from different sources, as can happen either through disease or malfunctioning of one or more of the organs involved, or when seemingly conflicting information is received, such as for example, during a ride on a helter-skelter.

In a Nutshell

To sum up the above, this is what happens in the ear during the process of hearing:

1) The sound impulses – which are transmitted in the air as vibrations – are received by the outer ear, the auricle serving as a not too efficient funnel that helps direct the vibrations into the external auditory meatus.

2) At the end of the external auditory meatus lies the eardrum and the sound impulses cause this membrane to vibrate.

3) On the inner side of the eardrum are the ossicles which together act as a chain along which the vibrations are amplified before being delivered to the oval window that separates the middle ear from the inner ear.

4) In the inner ear, the vibrations transmitted to the oval window from the ossicles are then transmitted via a fluid to the cochlea where the vibrations are transformed into nerve impulses.

The Vestibulocochlear Nerve

The sensory impulses generated in the inner ear are carried to the brain along the *vestibulocochlear nerve*. This is the eighth of 12 pairs of cranial nerves and is also known as the *auditory nerve* or *acoustic nerve*, and in medical texts is often indicated by the Roman numeral for eight, as 'VIII'.

The vestibulocochlear nerve has two branches:

1) The *cochlear nerve* is the nerve of hearing as it carries the impulses originating in the cochlea.

2) The *vestibular nerve* carries the impulses from the semicircular canals, utricles and saccules, that is information about balance, posture, and movement.

The auditory pathways connecting the ears to the brain also have a number of 'stations' along the way where nervous impulses are further processed. There are also interconnections between various corresponding stations in the left and the right pathways which allow for the comparison of information collected by the left and right ear, this comparison being part of the process through which the brain determines from which direction a particular sound came.

What Can Go Wrong?

Even from this simplified description of the hearing process, it's obvious that difficulties in hearing may be caused by a problem anywhere along its line of transmission. Things that can go wrong and impaire hearing, even temporarily include:

- ♦ In the outer ear, the channel may become blocked by wax, this physical obstruction stopping the vibrations from reaching the eardrum.
- ♦ The eardrum can be damaged and therefore unable to correctly receive the vibrations.
- ♦ Ossicles can also become damaged or fail to work properly, so reducing the degree of amplification their lever actions normally produce.
- ♦ Various diseases – more about these later in Chapter 5 – can interfere with, or interrupt, the transmission of sound vibrations.
- ♦ Additionally, all three parts of the ear can be become infected and inflamed, a condition called *otitis*, of which there are three main forms:

1) *Otitis externa* decribes inflammation of the outer ear. This occurs most frequently in swimmers and is therefore also known as *swimmer's ear*.

2) *Otitis media* is inflammation occuring in the middle ear and resulting from bacterial or viral infection. Treatment usually consists of antibiotics. Similar to this is *secretory otitis media* – also known as *glue ear* – a condition marked by the chronic accumulation of fluid in the middle ear and which is often treated by a relatively minor procedure during which a double-cuffed tube, called a *grommet*, is inserted in the eardrum to allow excess fluid to drain from the middle ear. Common symptoms of middle ear infection include moderate to severe pain and a high fever.

3) *Otitis interna* – also called *labyrinthitis* – refers to inflammation of the middle ear. Common symptoms include dizziness, an impaired sense of balance, and vomiting.

Naturally, any kind of ear infection needs prompt professional attention as without it the hearing may become permanently impaired.

Summing It Up

The process of hearing is a very intricate one, and metamorphosing air vibrations created by sound into nervous impulses the brain can interpret involves several quite separate stages, all of which need to be functioning properly to provide normal hearing.

In the next chapter, we will be looking at both what is meant by 'normal' hearing and how tinnitus interferes with this.

CHAPTER 3

Normal Hearing and Sound Perception

Before turning our attention to how tinnitus interferes with hearing, it's useful to begin by considering just what sounds someone with hearing that can be described as being 'normal' should be able to recognise and differentiate.

The three main fundamental characteristics of any given sound, and which determine what kind of sound it is, are its pitch, loudness and timbre, and the ability to clearly hear each of these constituent components varies greatly even in people considered to have normal hearing. Let us look at each of these components in turn:

Pitch

The pitch of a sound is how fast or slowly the object producing it vibrates – the faster the vibration, the higher the pitch of the sound will be. Generally, it can be said that the shorter or smaller the vibrating object is, the higher will be the pitch of the sounds it produces. For example, the strings producing the high notes found at the extreme right end of an acoustic piano's keyboard are much shorter than those producing the deep bass notes that are triggered by the keys at the extreme left of the keyboard. Equally, the notes available on a trumpet – which is comparatively small – will fall in a much higher range than those you can get from a tuba, a much larger instrument.

Naturally, in these days of synthesised sounds, the size of an electronic instrument no longer necessarily indicates whether it will be high- or low-pitched.

Pitch is measured by how many times the sound-producing source vibrates in a second, this measurement called cycles per second or *cps*, but also frequently expressed as 'Hertz', a term often abbreviated to 'Hz'. One Hertz represents one cycle per second; 10,000 Hertz means that the vibrations repeat 10,000 times a second. A thousand Hz is also often shown as one kHz, this abbreviation standing for one kiloHertz with 'kilo' denoting that the measurement is in units of a thousand.

Normally, humans can hear sounds occuring within the range of about 15 cycles per second to 20,000 cycles. However, it is common for the upper limit to become substantially reduced as you get older, the upper audibility mark falling perhaps to as little as half of that which you might have enjoyed when you were younger. By the way, the human ear can in fact usually detect sounds lower than 15 cycles per second, but what will be discerned will be an ill-defined rumble lacking any definite pitch. Sounds above 20,000 cycles are, however, totally inaudible for the vast majority of adults, although some rare individuals may be able to recognise them. Children can often hear sounds pitched as high as 40,000 cycles, but this ability begins to drop off by around 100 or so cycles a year once maturity has been reached.

Despite these limitations, the range of pitches audible to humans remains vast, covering in excess of 10 octaves. To put this in perspective, the range of a normal grand piano – one with 88 keys – is seven and a third octaves. Many animals, of course, can recognise much higher pitches and this is why the so-called 'silent' dog whistle works: the sound it makes is pitched higher than humans can hear – hence it's silent as far as they are concerned – but it still remains audible to a dog.

Just how the human detects pitch is not fully understood, but this is at least partly controlled by the cochlea, different parts of its basilar membrane appearing to be stimulated by different pitches. There is little doubt, however, that the auditory pathway and the brain itself play a major role in pitch recognition. So far, science has failed to come up with a totally credible explanation as to why some people have *perfect pitch* – that is the ability to pinpoint any note exactly – while others are relatively tone deaf and unable to distinguish with certainty between sounds that may be pitched as much as an octave apart.

Various experiments have proved that most people can improve their pitch recognition through aural or musical training, but that this usually only results in an improvement in recognising relative pitches — that is, whether one tone is higher or lower than another and how big the difference is between the two – rather than leading to eventual absolute pitch recognition, this remaining the dominion of those blessed with perfect pitch, an attribute usually present from birth, although its presence may not be recognised until much later in life.

Incidentally, it's worth noting that even those who are said to be totally tone deaf are rarely completely so, with most of them perfectly able to recognise great variations in pitch. Were it not so, then these people would have immense difficulties with the spoken word, which – even in English – relies at least partly upon rising or falling inflections to convery its full meaning, such as the pitch rising at the end of a sentence often indicating an unspoken but still very real question mark. Pitch is even more important in many other languages, notably Chinese, where a word may acquire totally different meanings according to the pitch at which it's spoken.

Loudness

While the loudness of a sound is determined by the amount of energy it releases – banging a drum with great force will create a louder sound than merely tapping it lightly – just how that loudness will be perceived by the human ear will also be affected by the pitch of the sound. Not all pitches are equal as far as the human ear is concerned and it will hear some more clearly – and therefore more loudly – than others.

The ear's sensitivity varies greatly over its hearing range, and while there are great variations from person to person, this is how it will operate in most people:

- The hearing will be most sensitive to sounds falling in

what is called the 'middle high tones range', this encompassing frequencies from about 1,000 to about 4,000 cycles per second. Man's ability to hear sounds in these frequencies is in fact so developed that were it any greater we would begin to audibly discern the movement of air particles themselves.

- Our hearing sensitivity drops off gradually below about 1,000 cycles. It is just as well that we cannot hear sounds below a certain pitch, our hearing would otherwise be under constant attack from low-frequency sounds produced within our own body, such as those resulting from bone and muscle movements.

- Hearing sensitivity also reduces sharply above the 4,000 cycles ceiling, and then does so much more rapidly than the drop-off in the lower bass. Incidentally, it is to deliberately counteract the ear's greater sensitivity to middle tones that hi-fis and many television sets have a 'tone control' you switch on when listening at low volume. What this control does is boost the relative volumes of sounds both in the lower bass and upper treble regions, so restoring the overall *perceived* balance more or less to that which you'd hear with the tone control switched off but with the main volume turned up higher.

To put the above ranges in perspective, the fundamental of the note middle C or *do* (located just to the left of the keyboard's centre) played on a correctly tuned piano will vibrate at 256 cycles. As the number of vibrations doubles or halves an octave higher or lower, this means that a standard piano's highest note – the top C at the extreme right – vibrates somewhat more than 4,000 times a second, and the instrument's lowest note – the A at the extreme left – vibrates 27.5 cycles a second, or nearly twice as fast as the average low pitch audibility threshold.

However, many sounds do not have a definite pitch like that produced by musical instruments and are instead a combination of many different pitches, these being so interwoven that no single specific pitch – or series of them – can be discerned. Sounds without specific pitch are known as *noises*, the word taking on a somewhat different meaning in this context, typical examples of which includes sounds like those made by boiling water or the clatter of horses' hooves.

Naturally, when the sound is a noise, the ear's sensitivity to pitch plays but little role in determining how loudly it is heard.

The range of loudness to which a healthy ear can respond is vast, the ratio having been calculated as a hundred million to one, meaning that the loudest recognisable sound may be a hundred thousand thousand times louder than the faintest one which can still be heard.

Loudness is expressed in *decibels* (often expressed as *dB*), a unit for indicating the relative intensity of sounds, and which results from a logarithmic calculation applied to a measurement of the variation that a given sound source creates in sound pressure of the air molecules. However, because as already explained, the human ear has varying sensitivity to different ranges of pitches, the standard decibel measurement is usually converted to a different form that takes this into account, known as dB(A). It is this unit of measurement that is used most commonly to express loudness levels as they relate to human hearing. To put these in perspective, here are the approximate dB(A) levels for some common sounds, all of these based upon the assumption that the listener is comparatively near to their source:

- Only just audible ambient sounds, such as those you might hear on a still day if you really listened for them – 10 dB(A).

- Whispered conversation – 40 dB(A).

- Conversation at normal loudness – 60 dB(A).

- Shouting loudly – 80 dB(A).

- Symphony orchestra during a loud passage – 100 dB(A).

- Jet aeroplane at full thrust, as during take-off – in excess of 120 dB(A).

- Firing of medium-calibre rifle – 160 dB(A).

Just where the thesholds of painful and/or harmful noise lie varies somewhat from person to person. Different experts also have conflicting views on this, but the following will serve as a point of reference:

- It's generally agreed that damage to hearing may result following prolonged exposure to sounds in excess of 90 decibels.

- Sounds in excess of 130 decibels are likely to be physically painful to endure as well as likely to cause damage.

It needs to be borne in mind, however, that the loudness of a sound is also related to the distance separating the listener from its source. In fact, scientists differentiate sharply between the intensity of a sound, this being a measurable physical quantity, and its loudness, this being the product of both the sound's intensity and how sensitive the ear is to it under the currently prevailing conditions.

Because our perception of loudness is also affected by our reaction to the kind of sound we're hearing, it can be difficult to state exactly at what level sound becomes obtrusive. For example, if you love Wagner's music you may well find the crescendo in the Ride of the Valkyries totally acceptable at 100 decibels. However, should the same loudness be produced by your neighbour's children playing the latest pop music, then you may well think of this as being excruciatingly painful.

Two other factors that affect just how 'loudly' we hear something:

1) The human brain generally does an excellent job in filtering out what we want to hear from that which is of no or little interest to us – for example, a mother may

well hear *her* child's voice more clearly than that of the other children when they're all singing at more or less the same volume in a choir.

2) When there are many sounds of varying volumes, the one with the consistently highest pitch will usually be heard most sharply, even though its volume may be lower than that of many of the other sounds. This phenomenon explains why - apart from what the sound engineers may have done with relative volumes when mixing a recording - the singer's voice (which is usually mainly in the treble) soars distinctively above that of the accompaniment (most of which will be in the bass and middle regions).

Timbre

The third major component by which a sound is identified, timbre, is that quality which makes a particular sound what it is or why a piano sounds like a piano and not a trumpet.

Virtually all sounds incorporate a number of what might be called sub-sounds, except that these additional sounds are in fact pitched higher than the one we hear most clearly. For example, if you strike the note middle C on a piano, the string struck by the hammer will vibrate at 256 cycles per second. However, apart from vibrating along its whole length, the string will also vibrate in halves. The two halves, of course, being exactly half the length of the whole string will therefore vibrate exactly twice as fast, producing a fainter but still discernible note sounding exactly an octave higher than the one being played, this latter being known as the fundamental. The creation of overtones doesn't stop at just halves because the piano's string will also vibrate in thirds, quarters and so on. Each of these subdivisions producing sounds that are pitched higher and higher until they are so high that they can no longer be heard by the human ear.

The sounds produced by the vibrations of only a part of the string are called *overtones, harmonics* or *partials,* and it is the relative volume of these that give an instrument its peculiar and distinctive sound. For example, a good piano will produce quite strong overtones throughout the audible range, but a clarinet will produce almost no overtones. Of course, it is not only musical instruments that produce overtones as these are literally part and parcel of most sounds, and one of the main reasons why we usually recognise them immediately for what they are. Because, by definition, overtones are pitched higher than their fundamental tones, it's quite common for some of these to fall in a range beyond that which we can hear. When that happens we may have difficulty in interpreting or understanding the source sound because we failed to capture enough of its overtones.

Another distinguishing mark of any sound is its *attack envelope*, a phrase that describes the manner in which the sound first manifests itself and then continues. Broadly speaking, there are two main types of attacks:

1) Percussive sounds are those which start off loudly and whose loudness then reduces rapidly. The piano and guitar are two common examples of instruments producing percussive sounds. Typical examples of non-musical percussive sounds include thunderclaps or the snap of a twig being broken.

2) Constant sounds are those whose volume alters but little while they are being produced, such as those coming from a flute or a church organ.

There is in fact a third major form of attack, one in which the sound starts off at low volume, then gradually increases in volume becoming louder and louder. Incidentally, many sounds incorporate more than one form of attack, with some aspects of the sound gradually rising in volume while others remain constant or diminish.

Speech, of course, according to what is being said and how it is being said can be either mainly percussive or constant, depending upon whether the speaker adopts a staccato or sing-song delivery. The manner of speech, apart from whether the speaker has a high or low voice, and speaks loudly or softly, will also influence the extent to which it may be heard clearly by someone whose hearing is less than perfect.

Sound Transmission

Of particular relevance to some forms of tinnitus is how sound can be transmitted. Generally, of course, the medium of transmission is the air, this responding to the vibrations created by the object making the sound, and the human ear is particularly suited to picking up airborne sounds.

Solids can, however, also act as excellent sound transmitters, one obvious example of this being the 'listening sticks' used by water company inspectors to detect leaks in underground pipes. Similarly, the human ear may hear sounds which are brought to it via the bones or the tissues of the body.

Liquids, too, are good sound transmitters, as evidenced by how electronic devices can track down submarines many miles away. Equally, the liquids in the body, the main one being blood, of course, can act as a conduit bringing sound sensations to the ear.

Summing It Up

All sounds - and therefore also all noises - consist of a number of different components, some of which may be more or less audible to a given individual, according to the state of his or her hearing. In the next chapter, we will be looking at the sounds associated with tinnitus, these generally - but not always - having no immediately obvious source.

CHAPTER 4

The Sounds of Tinnitus

In previous chapters we have seen how hearing works and what range of external sounds people with normal hearing would generally be able to hear.

While tinnitus is generally defined as 'noises heard in the ear in the absence of matching noises in the surrounding environment', this definition is not complete because it fails to take into account that tinnitus can also be the result of hearing sounds that do exist, although not necessarily in the environment but rather in the body itself.

There are, of course, many forms of tinnitus – and experts have created a wide variety of labels to define its various subdivisions – but essentially the disorder can be broadly classified as to whether its manifestation matches one or more of the following four main categories:

1) So-called *objective tinnitus* – some forms of which are also sometimes known as *pulsatile tinnitus* – occurs when the noises that are heard are real enough, although of a kind that most people do not hear. In these instances, the sounds can also be distinguished by observers and the source of the noises invariably lies within the body of the patient.

2) The phrase *subjective tinnitus* is generally used to describe a situation where the sounds heard by the patient, whether or not some of these may indeed still be the

result of what might yet be objective tinnitus were their source only more amenable to independent observation, are such that they are not audible to someone else, no matter what equipment may be used to try to detect them.

3) Additionally, tinnitus whether objective or subjective, can be further classified upon how much it affects the patient. If the symptoms of the tinnitus are so negligible or happen so rarely that the patient is most often unaware of their occurence and it causes him or her but little bother, then the condition is often described as *normal tinnitus*, a phrase that can also have a slightly different meaning as will be seen later.

4) On the other hand, the phrase *significant tinnitus* is, as you might expect from its first word, used to describe a situation in which the disorder is either frequent and/or noticeable enough to interfere to a greater or lesser extent with the sufferer's daily routine.

These general categories are not all mutually exclusive. However, tinnitus will be *either* objective or subjective; normal *or* significant, the four possible main permutations within these categories being tinnitus that is defined as:

1) Objective *and* normal. In this case, the noises can be detected by others, but they have hardly any effect on the patient.

2) Objective *and* significant. Once again, the noises can be independently confirmed, but their effect upon the patient is great enough to cause discomfort, distress, or worse.

3) Subjective *and* normal. The noises are only heard by the patient, but their effect remains minimal.

4) Subjective *and* significant. Again, only the patient can hear the noises and they have a considerable adverse effect on him or her.

Let us now look at the first two main types in greater detail:

Objective Tinnitus

The human body is a very busy place with all kinds of processes taking place all the time: the heart beats, the lungs expand and contract, foodstuffs make their way along the intestinal tract, joints move, blood courses through the veins and arteries, and so on. Many of these processes are far from silent and the sounds they make can often be readily detected by an independent observer using a stethoscope or other sound-amplification device at or near their source. However, under most circumstances, the vast majority of people remain blissfully unaware of the noises made by their own body as it goes about its routine tasks, this happening for two separate but interconnected reasons:

1) The sources of many of the body's internal sounds lie in areas that are well-insulated by surrounding muscles or other tissues, this insulation containing the vibrations created by the sounds and reducing their intensity outside the immediate area of their origin.

2) Despite the muffling effect of any insulation that may be present, many inner body sounds can still have enough energy to fall within the audible range by the time they reach the ears. However, because the brain has a marvellous ability to discard or ignore information that's not considered relevant at the moment, many – if not all – of these sounds will simply be 'filtered' out as though they didn't exist in the first place.

In fact, there is usually a third factor in play that also influences what body sounds are consciously perceived and which are not. As a generality, any such sound produced with regularity or more or less constantly will be ignored by the brain. It is, of course, very fortunate that this is the case because otherwise we would be conscious of hearing a thump with every heart beat or a whoosh of air whenever we breathed in or out.

Additionally, the brain's noise filtering mechanism also does an excellent job in recognising when a normal body noise suddenly changes for any reason. For example, someone with a slightly wheezy chest may be quite unaware of the sound this creates under normal circumstances, but should the wheeze change –although not necessarily become louder in absolute terms – then the brain can stop its filtering of this particular sound, so making it audible and thereby drawing the patient's attention to it. In some ways, making a previous inaudible sound perceivable can be compared to the protective aspect of pain, both of these serving to draw attention to something which has gone wrong or which is no longer behaving normally.

There are many possible sound sources within the body that can lead to objective tinnitus, the main ones including:

- The circulation. This has frequently been identified as a source of objective tinnitus, and particularly likely to be heard is the flow of blood through the bigger vessels in the head or, alternatively, through the very small arteries that supply the ear, most specifically those leading to the inner ear. As already mentioned, the heartbeats, too, can be a source of tinnitus noise. This kind of tinnitus is usually comparatively easy to diagnose because the noise will almost invariably vary and decrease in loudness in close synchronisation with the heartbeats. Incidentally, it needs to be noted that pulsatile tinnitus is by no means an indication that there is anything wrong as such with the circulation. Despite that, it would nevertheless be sensible to have your doctor do a general check-up. In passing, it's worth noting that liquids such as blood are an excellent medium for the transmission of sound vibrations.

- Next to the circulation, the skeleton is probably the most common source of sounds that result in objective tinnitus. Whereas all joints can potentially produce noise, the most likely offenders include bones in the jaw, neck, back, and shoulders. Rarely will tinnitus stem from a distant joint, such as a knee, although this can happen. Usually, but by no means always, investigation may discover that the 'guilty' bones have suffered some deterioration, such as by arthritis. Some people, of course, just have bones that 'click' more than the average, the sound produced being often loud enough to be heard quite clearly by anyone near them. Strangely enough, tinnitus seldom follows when the noise made by the bones is obviously audible.

- While muscles are a comparatively rare source of noises, those in the soft palate are an exception to this general rule, and tinnitus sounds have been clearly linked to their contraction.

Subjective Tinnitus

If no source can be identified for noise heard by the patient, then the disorder will be described as subjective tinnitus. However, it is important to keep in mind that this is a label that may not truly reflect the facts. For example, just because no inner body origin has been found to explain the noises, this is by no means absolute proof that there isn't such a source.

For example, some bodily sounds leading to tinnitus can be extremely difficult to locate, even with the help of today's very sensitive and sophisticated amplifying instruments. Obscure sounds like these would probably never have been identified a few decades ago when the equipment that can now track them down simply didn't exist, and the patient would have been diagnosed as having subjective tinnitus. It's therefore not unreasonable to speculate that there are possibly further inner body sounds that are so faint that their detection remains beyond the power of modern gadgetry, but that these may be identified by even more powerful equipment in years to come. Should this happen, then it's very possible that many a diagnosis will have to be revised, with cases previously lebelled as being subjective tinnitus then falling clearly in the objective tinnitus category.

Additionally, the phrase subjective tinnitus should never be interpreted as meaning that the noises are *imagined*, as almost certainly there is indeed a physical cause for them, even if that cause is not itself producing sound but instead leads to what can only be called the sensation of sound elsewhere. For example, as will be explained more fully later when we look at the causes of tinnitus, the disorder can often be linked to damage in some area of the body, this most commonly, of course, being one that is part of the hearing system. While the area that's damaged doesn't itself *make* a sound, it may nevertheless create nerve impulses that either the ear or the brain mistakenly recognises as sound impulses. Just like those of objective tinnitus, the origins of the subjective variety can often be traced to specific physical malfunction or damage.

It's worth stressing the point made above because unfortunately the phrase 'hearing noises in the head' – which is commonly used to describe tinnitus, even by people afflicted by the disorder – all too readily lends itself to being misinterpreted as suggesting that the noises aren't 'real', that they're creations of the mind instead of being symptoms of something gone physically awry. The sensation of hearing sounds is real enough, even though the source of these sensations may itself not be a sound-producer, in that it doesn't create sound vibrations but, instead sets off impulses or signals that are eventually perceived as sounds by the brain.

Significant or Not?

The dividing line between normal and significant tinnitus is one that can be blurred at times, because the extent to which someone may be affected by the disorder depends more upon his or her individual reaction to the noises than upon how loud they are or appear to be.

Statistical surveys of tinnitus sufferers have often shown that there can be quite a discrepancy between how loud or constant a sufferer may say the noises are, and how much he or she is affected by them. It would be totally wrong to assume that simply because a sufferer describes the noises he or she hears as faint or occasional that they therefore are of not great significance. On the contrary, some of the people most distressed by tinnitus report the sounds they hear as being quite faint. Conversely, other patients who report relatively loud tinnitus noises say that they are not bothered greatly by them.

This lack of correlation between the loudness of tinnitus and how much it affects the patient occurs in both subjective and objective tinnitus. It is the very fact that loudness doesn't necessarily bring proportionate distress that has provided a very important clue as to how tinnitus that cannot be cured can still be considerably alleviated, as will be explained fully in later chapters.

Naturally, how frequently the noises are heard has a great bearing upon their impact. As might be expected, if the tinnitus occurs but rarely, then it's usually much easier to bear than if it is constant or virtually so. However, interestingly enough, some sufferers from intermittent tinnitus have said that they thought it might bother them less if it were constant. One patient explained this view as follows: "It's bad enough when I hear the noises, but what is worse is not knowing when they may strike again. When I'm free of the noises for a good while, I begin to hope that I've been cured. Then the sounds come back, and that is such a letdown that I wish they had never gone away at all if they weren't going to disappear forever."

Just when and for how long the sounds of tinnitus are heard by sufferers varies just as greatly as the nature of the sounds perceived. At one extreme, some patients say that their noises are with them all the time, even 'hearing' them while they are asleep; others say that the sounds only occur rarely, perhaps as infrequently as every few months. Most commonly, however, patients say the noises do abate now and then, sometimes for lengthy periods, there usually being no obvious pattern to their presence or absence.

Finally, it has to be noted that whether tinnitus is significant or not in a given individual is not a situation that is graven in stone. Tinnitus that began as 'normal' may worsen into becoming 'significant'; more rarely, the reverse may also happen, and when it does it's usually because the sufferer has learned to adapt to their tinnitus rather than the condition having improved to any great extent. Naturally, depending upon its cause, tinnitus can also respond dramatically to treatment, so reducing it to a level where it can no longer be called significant.

Incidentally, the phrase 'normal tinnitus' is also used to describe that very temporary form of the disorder that just about everyone now and then experiences in a comparatively minor way. People who do not have tinnitus as such are still quite likely to hear 'noises in their head' for a little while after having been exposed to very loud sounds, such as having spent the evening in a disco. That kind of tinnitus, if that is what it really is, does however usually clear up of its own accord within minutes, or at worst within an hour or so, although there is some evidence to indicate that repeated experiences of this kind are likely to predispose to the development of true tinnitus later.

The Noises of Tinnitus

While almost any kind of sound may be experienced by a tinnitus sufferer, there are some that patients report time and time again, the more common of these including:

- Ringing sounds, ranging from those resembling a telephone's shrill ring to more sonorous bell-like noises. Ringing noises, of course, are classically associated with tinnitus, it having been frequently described as 'living with ringing in your ears' or the 'ringing disease'.

- Ill-defined sounds, somewhat like those made by a babbling brook.

- A hissing noise, usually quite high-pitched, resembling that made by the steam emerging from the spout of a kettle coming to the boil.

- A buzzing noise, rather like that of swarming, flying insects.

- Humming sounds in all their possible permutations, such as hums that sound like a muffled choir or like the background noise produced by a radio that's turned on but not tuned into a station.

- Clicking sounds of all kinds – including those like the tapping of the keys of an old-fashioned typewriter or the sounds made by a hot car engine as it cools down after having been switched off. The clicks may either follow a pattern, recurring at fairly consistent intervals, or be totally random. Irregular clicking noises, of course, are often associated with objective tinnitus stemming from noises made by joints in the body.

- Whistling noises of all kinds – ranging from human whistling to mechanical whistles, with both the pitch and the volume usually remaining fairly constant.

- A throbbing noise, usually quite low in pitch.

- A noise that resembles a growl, except that it doesn't come to a natural end but continues indefinitely.

- Tweet-like sounds, a bit like birds chirping.

Extensive though the above list is, it only covers a fraction of the kind of noises that tinnitus sufferers have reported. In fact, it can be safely said that if you think of a sound, any sound, then it's almost certain that someone somewhere experiences that sound as tinnitus. To further demonstrate just how varied tinnitus can be, here are some of the more unusual sounds reported as they were originally described by patients:

- Sometimes I think that what I'm hearing is the noise made by the earth as it turns on its axis.

- I keep hearing musical notes. All the notes have a very definite pitch and vary in length, just like those in a composition, but they never develop into anything even remotely like a tune.

- It's as though a group of very shrill-voiced children are shouting and yelling as they play their games in my head.
- I can't describe the sound I hear, other than it's very deep, very ominous, and almost threatening.
- It's just like being in the middle of what I imagine a railway shunting yard to be like: the clatter of heavy steel wheels on rails; the hissing and puffing of steam engines; and the clanking of freight wagons.

Although many people with tinnitus refer to noises that *sound* like those made by human voices, few indeed report these noises as voices, generally choosing to describe them instead as being 'voice-like'. Yet some patients do speak of hearing distinct voices, speaking words that now and then are recognisable and which may or may not make some sort of sense.

Some experts have speculated that voices are heard by more tinnitus sufferers than has been revealed by various research projects. The reason for this being that patients may be very reluctant to admit to hearing voices because this symptom is so strongly associated with certain forms of mental illness. However, judging by what has been reported by tinnitus sufferers who have said they heard voices, the kind of words spoken by the inner voices of tinnitus sufferers are very different from those heard by mental patients: tinnitus patients generally appear to hear random words, as though they were eavesdropping on a conversation, but only hearing part of it; people with mental problems usually report that the voices they hear are very clear, very definite, often speaking with great authority, as well as issuing commands and demands.

Stereo or Mono?

Depending upon its causes, the noises of tinnitus may be heard by the patient in both ears or only one. In fact, as we'll see later, which of these applies can be an important clue in determining what the underlying cause may be. Occasionally, the noises may shift from one ear to the other.

Much more rarely, a patient may report that they 'sense' the noises rather than 'hear' them, the sensation then usually appearing to be coming from somewhere within the head.

Most commonly, tinnitus sufferers say that they hear only one kind of noise, although some of its characteristics may change at different times, become louder or softer, shriller or deeper, yet essentially remaining the same. Some patients, however, experience a whole gamut of different sounds, either separately or at times mixed together in total cacophony.

Summing It Up

Tinnitus can manifest itself in an incredible variety of ways, with the possible permutations of its symptoms being virtually infinite. Although, according to the symptoms it produces, the disorder can be classified into several main categories, a patient's individual experience of it is almost certainly unique.

In the next chapter, we will be looking more closely at the various causes of tinnitus and also at how the risk of developing it can be reduced.

CHAPTER 5

The Causes of Tinnitus and How to Prevent It

Before looking at the causes of tinnitus, it is useful to first of all consider exactly what is meant by the word 'cause' in this context.

For example, it is known that tinnitus often follows prolonged exposure to very loud sounds, these eventually damaging parts of the hearing system. But which is the true cause of the resultant tinnitus? Is it the damage to the ears – or is it the exposure to the sounds that brought on the damage in the first place? There is no simple answer to that question and one could argue forever as to which factor should be judged to be the cause of the tinnitus under those circumstances. Interesting though such an argument may be from an academic view point, its outcome would not be of great help to someone seeking to reduce his or her risk of developing tinnitus, except for drawing the obvious conclusion that loud sounds are best avoided.

In this chapter, we will therefore use the word 'cause' as it's generally understood by most people, something which is seen as bringing about something else, the something else in this instance naturally being tinnitus. At the same time, we will be paying particular attention to those causes whose impact can be lessened by preventative measures.

In some cases it will be possible to clearly establish a cause for the tinnitus, such as when it's due to the taking of certain medications or because the ear canal has become blocked by compacted earwax. In most instances, however, the immediate cause will be less obvious and may often be a matter of conjecture. One recent massive survey of nearly 1,000 tinnitus sufferers asked them what they *believed* might have caused or triggered off their tinnitus:

- Nearly a quarter of the respondents believed that their tinnitus was due to previous exposure to loud noises.

- Just under a quarter attributed their problems to stress.

- One out of every five sufferers said that their tinnitus was caused by having catarrh or being asthmatic.

Other 'causes' frequently mentioned by patients include a history of hearing disorders (nearly 15 per cent), the accumulation of earwax (six per cent), and a previous operation not involving the ear (also six per cent).

Causes that came up much more rarely included migraines and headaches, as well as having suffered a heavy blow on the head.

When the same patients were asked to list events that occured more or less at the same time as the tinnitus first became noticeable, the answers suggested other possible triggering factors:

- One in eight said that the onset of the disorder followed having a bad cold or influenza.

- Roughly ten per cent said that loud noise had brought on the tinnitus; an equal number linked it to either Meniere's disease or vertigo. Somewhat fewer patients said that their tinnitus began when they became partially deaf.

- Other events mentioned frequently included an ear operation or infection of the ear (nearly nine per cent), medical treatment by drugs or injection for another problem (also nearly nine per cent), a blow to the ear or the head (eight per cent), preceeding illness (nearly four per cent). Interestingly, in this context, stress was only mentioned by somewhat less than four per cent.

Events mentioned by relatively few sufferers included having their ears syringed to remove compacted wax or having had dental treatment that involved drilling (two per cent), pregnancy (less than one per cent), and the menopause (also less than one per cent).

Additionally, just over 11 per cent of the respondents reported that their tinnitus started without any warning whatever, and they were unable to link its onset to any specific event.

Naturally, these statistics, based as they are on the patients' personal view of their experiences, do not *prove* that the events reported actually caused the tinnitus, but they are certainly indicative. In many instances, of course, the cited events are those which can be proven to cause tinnitus, such as excessive noise or the accumulation of earwax. Other events mentioned as causes are less susceptible to proof, such as stress or general illness.

The truth is that the cause of the disorder remains largely unknown in many cases of tinnitus. Yes, there may be some very strong pointers suggesting what brought it on, but absolute proof of the root-cause will still often remain elusive.

Despite the above, there are, of course, many causes that can be clearly and unequivocally identified as such, and we will now look at the main ones.

Noise

The damage that noise can cause to hearing can be divided into two major categories:

1) Damage that is the result of a single incident involving an extremely high level of noise. Typical examples of this are explosions or gunfire. Usually, but by no means always, the hearing impairment will manifest itself relatively soon, if not immediately. Extremely loud noises can in fact totally destroy the organ of Corti in the inner ear, reducing it to fragments. Even death can be caused by a loud enough noise.

2) Damage that follows repeated and prolonged exposure to noise, such as working in a noisy environment or

> spending most evenings in a discotheque. This sort of damage usually takes a long time – years, even decades – before its effect becomes noticeable. Once again, the organ of Corti is usually affected with some of the hairs, cells having been destroyed, or the hairs themselves distorted, by the cumulative effect of noise exposure.

Naturally, it is not uncommon for hearing damage to have become adversely affected by *both* kinds of damage or, for it to be less than obvious what kind of damage led to the impairment. For example, someone who served in the Armed Forces and at the time was exposed to the sound of gunfire may later work in an automobile asssembly plant. Should his hearing start to fail some time thereafter, it would indeed be difficult to state with any certainty the extent to which either of these factors were to blame. One of the difficulties with linking cause and effect in many types of hearing problems is that the disorder is often insidious, worsening ever so slightly and gradually, that it may take years before the patient becomes acutely aware that something is wrong.

Naturally, the way to prevent noise-induced hearing damage is to avoid noises loud enough to cause it, something that isn't always possible. However, these suggestions may help:

- ♦ Wear the right kind of ear protectors when operating noisy machines.
- ♦ If your work environment is a noisy one, be sure that all governmental regulations about maximum noise levels are obeyed.
- ♦ When listening to personal radios or cassette players through earphones, always switch on the equipment and reduce the volume before placing the headset over your ears. Putting on the earphones first and then switching on may unleash a sudden blast of high-intensity sound.
- ♦ If rock concerts – or other equally loud entertainments

– are your pleasure, avoid being too near the stage – the nearer you are, the greater the possible injury inflicted on your ears.

- If you are persistently and unavoidably exposed to loud noise – such as being a train driver – then make sure that you have your hearing monitored at regular intervals. And should you ever experience the slightest ringing in your ears, then take this as a warning sign that it might be the first indication of tinnitus, and immediately seek professional advice.

The Ageing Process

Even without the harmful effects of excessive noise, it is a sad fact that hearing normally deteroriates with the passing of the years. As was noted previously, what happens most commonly is that high-pitched sounds are no longer heard as clearly as before, if at all. Initially, this loss usually doesn't matter all that much for most people because the sounds they can no longer hear are usually not all that important to them. However, as the condition progresses and begins to affect the middle range – that region between about 500 and 3,000 Hz, where most speech falls – then there may be difficulty in recognising words or parts of them. In spoken English most consonants are usually pitched higher than the vowels and therefore the first noticeable sign of hearing loss may well be an occasional inability to hear consonants. Another classical indication of hearing loss is difficulty in separating sounds, such as having trouble hearing one voice from the others in general conversation involving several people.

It can be difficult to differentiate between what might be called 'normal' hearing loss, this due to the ageing process, and that which has been exacerbated for other reasons, but as a generality this is what can be expected, this being subject to great variations from individual to individual:

- The symptoms of normal hearing loss seldom become apparent before the age of sixty years, although it will in fact be the result of a very slow process that will have been at work for decades. This hearing loss, like that from many other causes, is invariably due to the degeneration of the hair cells and the nerve fibres in the organ of Corti, the damage being restricted to that area where the higher tones are perceived.

- Once the deterioration has become noticeable, it will appear to progress more rapidly, and relatively few people older than seventy will still be able to distinguish sounds much higher than the highest note on a piano.

Loudness Recruitment

A curious effect known as 'loudness recruitment' normally accompanies hearing impairment that's due to inner ear damage. Recruitment is characterised as follows:

- The hearing will be poor when the sounds are of low intensity, intensity of course also being related to the distance separating the listener from the source.
- The hearing will improve drastically as the intensity of the sound increases, this improvement being much greater than that which would normally accompany the increase in intensity.

In other words, what happens is that someone with loudness recruitment experiences larger variations in the volume of what he or she hears than those actually present in the sounds. Just why this phenomenon occurs is not fully understood. Some experts put it down as the brain increasing the ear's sensitivity across the currently audible range of frequencies to make up for the loss of those frequencies which are no longer heard clearly. Useful a stratagem though recruitment may appear to be at first glance, it in fact creates more problems than it solves because it over-emphasises the normal volume variations in ordinary speech and, can make it all the more difficult for an affected person to hear it properly. Recruitment is one of the reasons why if you slightly raise your voice when speaking to someone whose hearing you know to be impaired, you may then be accused of shouting at him or her.

Recruitment is also believed to be a frequent contributor to tinnitus, the increased sensitivity it creates in some frequencies leading to the hearing of sounds whose level would otherwise have been too low to have been noticed. Although recruitment is difficult to explain, it can be compared to what happens when you turn up the volume control on a hi-fi unit: as the overall volume from the speakers increase, it also becomes easier to distinguish any background hiss or static that may be present. Similarly, some forms of tinnitus are believed to be the result of the ear's 'volume control' being turned up so high that previously ignored background noises are now discerned.

Earwax

Earwax – its medical name is *cerumen* – normally plays a key role in protecting our hearing from damage, but as everyone knows, too much of a good thing can soon become a bad one, and earwax is no exception to that rule.

Under normal circumstances, earwax – which is produced by modified sweat glands in the skin lining our outer ear canals – fulfills several important purposes:

- It provides a barrier against possible infection, trapping dust and small foreign particles.
- It helps keep the ear canals supple, while at the same time repelling excess moisture.
- It also acts as a 'trap' for any insect that might invade the outer ear, the intruder getting stuck onto the wax before it can reach the eardrum where it could do greater damage.

Despite earwax's beneficial role, it can be a source of hearing problems when for one reason or another it either accumulates or becomes compacted or hardened. Generally, the ears will clear themselves of wax, but occasionally this automatic process will fail to do a good enough job and the wax then can cause deafness and/ or tinnitus. Fortunately, both conditions can be cured by the removal of the compacted or hardened wax, something that can be accomplished in several ways. However, before looking at these, a warning: **Never introduce any instrument whatsoever in your ears in an effort to clear wax.**

There are three good reasons for this admonition: firstly, probing about in the ear is almost certainly going to compress what wax there may be there, making it all the less likely that Nature's own way will eventually clear it; secondly, whatever you use, be it a cottonbud stick or the wetted corner of a towel, it is likely to irritate the ear canal's lining, making it secrete more wax than normal and so compounding the problem; finally, there's a good possibility that you can rupture your eardrum!

Although there are various across-the-counter preparations you can buy to help shift recalcitrant wax, truly the best thing to do if you have a hearing problem you believe is caused by wax is to consult your doctor. That way you will not only almost certainly receive confirmation of your self-diagnosis but also have any other possibility eliminated. What's more, your doctor will arrange to have the wax removed safely by a nurse.

There are several methods of removing wax:

- Still most commonly used is an ear syringe, an instrument consisting of a cylindrical metal body with a spout at one end and a plunger at the other. The syringe is filled with warm water, the spout applied to the ear, and the nurse pushes the plunger, propelling the water into the ear where its pressure loosens and washes away the wax.

- A more modern version of the old-fashioned ear syringe is an instrument remarkably similar to the water picks used to massage gums or clear away food debris between the teeth. Like the dental pick, this kind of syringe uses a jet of pulsating water, the intensity of which can be controlled. One big advantage of this method is that the pick is small enough so it can be observed while it does its work in the ear, therefore allowing the operator to direct it exactly where it's needed.

- Perhaps the best way of removing wax is the 'dry method' in which a delicate probe is used to prise it away and break it up, the fragments then being sucked up by a vacuum pump. Unfortunately, this method is not generally available at most local surgeries.

The following tips can help prevent wax from building up to the point where it becomes troublesome:

- Put a couple of drops of slightly warmed - not hot! - olive oil in each ear about once a month to stop the wax from forming a solid plug. The easiest way to do this is to stand in front of a mirror, tilt your head to the side, then use an eyedropper to let the oil fall into the ear. Place a little bit of cotton wool (make sure this is big enough not to be able to actually enter the ear canal but just jammed at its opening) in the outer rim of the ear for about twenty minutes to stop the oil from coming out before it hass done its work.

- Water entering the ear can swell any wax there and compact it. To avoid this happening: wear earplugs when swimming; plug your ears with cotton wool before showering or shampooing; make sure that your shower spray is never aimed directly at your ear opening.

While earwax can be a direct cause of tinnitus, it has also been suggested that syringing compacted wax can set off the problem, as many tinnitus sufferers have reported that their problems began just after their ears were syringed. Despite the vast amount of anecdotal evidence to support this idea, medical experts do not believe that syringing does lead to tinnitus, offering two possible explanations as to why the two may appear to be linked as cause and effect:

- The patient's hearing was already susceptible to tinnitus before the wax build-up and the disorder would have developed eventually in any case, its onset shortly after syringing being probably coincidental.
- Wax – especially if it has collected on the eardrum rather than merely blocking the ear canal elsewhere – can create tinnitus. Once someone experiences the disorder, he or she become more aware of its symptoms and, because of this increased awareness may now hear faint tinnitus that previously went unnoticed, although it may have existed long before there was a problem with earwax.

Otosclerosis

This is a primarily hereditary disorder that while often developing from late adolescence onward, generally manifests itself in later life when extra bone formation occurs in the inner ear, this overgrowth leading to restricted movement of the ossicles in the middle ear, the stapes usually being most severely affected, even to the extent of becoming fixed to the oval window. Unless treated, the condition is progressive, leading to gradually deeper deafness as the transmission of sound vibrations becomes more and more impeded.

Tinnitus frequently accompanies developing otosclerosis, although it is also possible for a patient to have the two conditions simultaneously, with each being due to quite independent and separate causes. If tinnitus is present as a result of otosclerosis, then the noise it produces will usually be low-pitched.

Apart from tinnitus, another common symptom of otosclerosis includes hearing sounds as being 'distorted', this distortion occuring long before loss of hearing becomes noticeable. The disorder is also frequently marked by patients reporting that their hearing is at its worst in quiet surroundings and appears more acute in noisy environments.

Comparatively rarely, the condition may also be marked by vertigo.

Apart from using hearing aids to enhance the impaired sound recognition, otosclerosis can also be treated by *stapedectomy*, a surgical procedure in which the stapes is replaced by a small plastic piston that performs the same job. Stapedectomies are usually very successful in restoring hearing, but they do not always clear up any tinnitus that may be present.

Meniere's Disease

Usually affecting only one ear and relatively uncommon in people under the age of 50 years, Meniere's disease - also known as *Meniere's syndrome* - is a disorder of the inner ear, its main symptoms including deafness, tinnitus, vertigo, and vomiting.

The symptoms are brought on by a substantial increase in the fluid in the semi-circular canals in the inner ears that help control balance and determine body position. The extra fluid damages the canals and, at times, also the cochlea, so interfering with sound perception and sometimes causing tinnitus. Unlike most other forms of deafness, the one that marks Meniere's normally involves low frequency sounds, the loss usually being accompanied by loudness recruitment.

Most commonly, the first sign of the disorder is a sudden attack of vertigo, this at times being so severe that the patient may collapse. Attacks are occasionally preceded for a few days by discomfort or pain in the ear or tinnitus. How long attacks last and how often they occur varies greatly, but in most cases the deafness and tinnitus will persist between them.

The cause of Meniere's remains unknown in about half of the cases, the others being attributed to a variety of factors, including food allergy, congenital or acquired syphilis, low activity of the pituitary, adrenal or thyroid glands, diabetes, viral infection, and high blood pressure.

If a cause can be identified, then treatment will usually be addressed to rectifying the underlying problem. Other forms of treatment include drugs - notably *betahistine dihydrochloride,* trade name *Serc* - which can lead to a reversal of the symptoms in the early stages of the disease. Left untreated, the condition invariably worsens, although the vertigo and the tinnitus may disappear as the deafness deepens or becomes total.

High Blood Pressure

There is a considerable amount of debate about the extent to which hypertension – that is having blood pressure that is chronically higher than normal for someone of the same age – contributes to tinnitus. Certainly, if the hypertension leads to Meniere's disease, then the link with tinnitus is proven. In many other instances, however, the connection is more tenuous, consisting mainly of the observation that many patients with tinnitus also have hypertension and that the former may improve when the latter is treated.

Whatever may be the effects of hypertension on tinnitus in general, there are aspects of it that clearly can influence tinnitus in two very specific ways:

1) Blood being pushed around the body at higher than normal pressure may create more intense sounds. If the tinnitus is of the pulsatile variety, that is its noises occur in synchronisation with the pulse, then it seems likely that the louder the sounds made by the blood are, the more likely these will be heard as tinnitus.

2) The tinnitus may be the result of the blood being pushed that much harder through the very fine arteries that supply the ear itself.

If you have tinnitus for no other obvious reason and are also hypertensive, then it may well be that your hearing disorder will improve if you take steps to reduce your blood pressure. Equally, it seems logical – although not proven – that following a lifestyle that reduces the risk of hypertension may also reduce your chances of getting tinnitus.

Although it is beyond the scope of this book to go deeply into hypertension, here are some suggestions that can help either prevent it or reduce it if already present:

- Although severe hypertension may need drug treatment, milder instances of it can respond remarkably well and rapidly to making simple lifestyle adjustments, these including keeping your weight down, getting more exercise, reducing your alcohol intake, and stopping smoking.

- Mental stress and anxiety are strongly linked to raised blood pressure and these can also be factors influencing how much tinnitus affects you. Simple programmes to reduce stress and promote relaxation are described in detail later in this book, and these can provide a dual benefit by helping you cope better with tinnitus as well as reducing your blood pressure if it's too high.

It needs to be added that apart from being a factor in tinnitus, hypertension also creates a substantially higher risk of eventually developing heart problems, having a stroke, and can also lead to many other serious diseases – all good reasons why it's a good idea to have your blood pressure checked regularly by your doctor.

Tinnitus as a Symptom of Another Disorder

Tinnitus is also associated with a number of other diseases or conditions. Not uncommonly, tinnitus is the 'presenting symptom' in these cases, that is, it is the problem that brought the patient to seek medical help, or 'present' themself, in the first instance. While a complete list of disorders that can include tinnitus as one of its symptoms would be virtually endless, here are some brief notes about some of the main ones:

TUMOURS – The word 'tumour' merely indicates an abnormal swelling, usually due to an abnormal growth of tissues, in or on part of the body and does not by any means indicate cancer, as a tumour may be benign or malignant.

There is one kind of benign – that is non-cancerous – tumour called an *acoustic neuroma* that creates tinnitus because it occurs in the fibrous sheet that covers the eighth cranial nerve, the one that links the inner ear with the brain. Tinnitus stemming from this cause is also usually accompanied by vertigo because a branch of the affected nerve also carries the signals from the organs of balance in the ear. Almost invariably only one ear is affected. While acoustic neuromas can be removed by surgery, this procedure only produces noticeable relief from any associated tinnitus in about half the cases.

THYROID PROBLEMS – The thyroid gland is charged with maintaining the body's metabolic rate and it does this by releasing various hormones. Both an over-active or an under-active thyroid – these leading respectively to *hyperthyroidism* and *hypothyroidism* – can be marked by tinnitus.

DIABETES – Already mentioned as a possible cause of Meniere's disease, diabetes is a condition in which the body's cells fail to properly take in glucose as fuel due to a shortage of insulin. Various researchers have pointed out that a much higher proportion than might have been statistically expected of tinnitus sufferers are also diabetics.

MULTIPLE SCLEROSIS (also known as *disseminated sclerosis*) – A chronic disease of the central nervous system, multiple sclerosis mainly affects young and middle-aged adults. The disease, whose underlying cause remains unknown, causes damage in the myelin sheaths surrounding nerves in the brain and the spinal cord. If the disorder spreads to nerves linking the brain and the ears, then tinnitus may follow.

MENINGITIS – Tinnitus may be the first symptom of meningitis, an inflammation of the meninges (the three connective tissue membranes that line the skull and vertebral canal) caused by viral or bacterial infection. Other common symptoms of meningitis include severe headache, rigidity of muscles, depleted appetite, and, in severe cases, convulsions. Treatment varies according to the cause, with bacterial meningitis responding to antibiotics and sulphonamides, while viral meningitis requires prolonged bed rest.

HEAD INJURIES - As might be expected, injuries to the head - especially if surgery was required to deal with them - are often linked to the immediate or later onset tinnitus. Because of the number of variables involved, it is often less than clear whether the tinnitus is a direct result of the injury or whether there already was a predisposition to the disorder.

DRUGS - Medications used to treat a variety of ailments have also been shown to produce tinnitus as a side-effect in susceptible people. For more information, see Chapter 7.

Summing It Up

Tinnitus can be due to a wide-ranging variety of causes and it can be difficult to identify which one may be responsible in a given case. In the next chapter, we will discover how tinnitus is diagnosed, its treatment then being matched to its cause.

CHAPTER 6

The Diagnosis of Tinnitus and Medical Treatment for It

Purists could argue that tinnitus is a symptom rather than a disorder or disease as such, and the noises associated with it are merely an indication that something is wrong, that something being the underlying disorder. However, in general usage the word 'tinnitus' covers a much wider area than just that, denoting both symptom and disorder as required. The distinction can, however, be an important one because although one might say that someone is suffering from tinnitus, the fact may be that the patient has Meniere's disease and tinnitus is merely one of its symptoms.

While on the subject of definitions, it's perhaps just as well to clarify what 'diagnosis' means in its strict definition when it describes the whole process involved in determining the nature of a disorder, by taking into account many factors, the main ones including:

- Symptoms – these are problems of which the patient is aware, such as being troubled by hearing noises which do not obviously match, or are caused by, sounds in the environment. It is, of course, the presence of one or more symptoms that normally leads a patient to seek medical help.

- Signs – these are indications pointing to a particular disorder and which are recognised by the doctor but which are not apparent to, or recognised by, the patient. For example, someone complaining of hearing noises may not be aware that there is an accumulation of wax in their ear, but the doctor will spot this as a sign of the underlying problem. Incidentally, this particular example illustrates that a given occurence is not necessarily either a symptom or a sign. Had the hypothetical patient above noticed the wax themself and reported this to their doctor, then the presence of wax would have been a symptom instead of a sign.

- Medical background – naturally, what problems a patient may have had in the past can provide a vital clue to determining what it is exactly that's bothering them now, especially if the current difficulty appears to be a repetition of a previous similar episode. To continue with the example above, if the patient with compacted wax complained of diminished hearing but then also revealed that their ears had to be syringed in the past, then it would be pretty obvious where the origin of the problem was likely to be found. Of course, the clues that may be revealed by taking a patient's medical history are seldom that obvious and usually require a great deal more detective work to unravel.

- The results of laboratory or other tests – what tests will be required will of course be determined by the findings of the initial examination, during which a tentative diagnosis may already have been reached in many cases, the tests being requested mainly for confirmation. In other instances, tests will be needed to exclude certain possible causes of the symptoms, so reducing the number of those that still need to be considered. When tinnitus is the main or only symptom, tests of various kinds often play a major role in making a *differential diagnosis*, this being a diagnosis of a condition whose symptoms and/or signs also mark other conditions. As we saw in the previous chapter, tinnitus can be the first symptom of a number of disorders and it's obviously of vital importance to find out which one is the underlying problem.

Naturally, not every case of tinnitus is investigated in such depth, as in many instances it is very clear just what the matter is and what can be done about it. It is unfortunately only too true that not all tinnitus sufferers get all the help that's available, this at times being due to their own failure to press hard enough for expert attention.

To start at the very beginning of the medical process as it were, someone experiencing tinnitus will almost invariably turn to their family doctor in the first instance.

With tinnitus - as with so many other complaints - general practitioners have the unenviable task of acting as a clearing house, determining and judging whether a particular case lies within their own competence or whether it needs to be attended to by a specialist. While there are no hard and fast guidelines to cover this, it would be most unusual for a GP not to refer a patient with ongoing and marked tinnitus - unless this were due to compacted earwax or some other similarly obvious and curable cause - to the Ear, Nose and Throat (ENT) department of the local hospital. Having said that, it also needs to be noted that some GPs do have to be coaxed somewhat before they will provide a referral, especially when the condition is mild. For those sufferers who might be reluctant to put pressure on their family doctor, it's well worth remembering that a hearing problem that remains less than fully diagnosed, and therefore not treated as effectively as it might be, can only be expected to become worse, a curable condition possibly becoming an incurable one with the passage of time. It is therefore sensible to insist on being referred to a specialist if your tinnitus fails to improve after treatment provided by your GP.

Preparing for a Consultation

Having been referred to an ENT specialist, the chances are that you may well have to wait quite a while before your appointment. In the meantime, it is quite a good idea to keep a note of how your symptoms are progressing on a day-to-day basis as this information can sometimes help identify the cause of your troubles, such as, for example, whether the noises are triggered by specific events, these often but not invariably being sounds.

It can also be useful to jot down other things which may or may not be connected with your tinnitus, such as what other health problems you experience, what medications you take for these, and also whether there are any periods of high stress or bouts of anxiety and/ or depression. Of particular importance, of course, is anything which occurs shortly before or at the same time that your tinnitus is at its worst. Equally important can be anything that seems to alleviate the severity of the problem.

What Happens During a Consultation

Although individual consultants will have their own preferred approach, you can expect your initial examination to proceed more or less along set lines. Beginning with an interview, then a physical examination and a brief check of some basic hearing functions. Followed perhaps by some more questions after which you may be offered a diagnosis, this possibly only being a tentative one that will be subject to confirmation by further tests.

The Questions You're Likely to be Asked

After having taken down some general details about you, the consultant will then ask specific questions relating to your problems, the areas covered at this time including:

- Your general medical history, including possibly that of your family as well.
- What medications you're taking currently and which ones you've taken previously. Medications in this context includes both prescribed medicines and those you've bought without a prescription.
- If any jobs you've ever held might have created a special risk of hearing damage.

Then come questions dealing directly with the problem, such as:

- How long have you experienced the difficulties?

- Are both ears affected? And if so, to the same extent? If only one ear is affected, which one? Or is the tinnitus 'sensed' elsewhere than in the ears? Is there or has there been discharge from the ears? If so, what form did it take?

- Are the hearing difficulties accompanied by any pain or discomfort? If so, all the time or only occasionally? How severe is the pain?

- Are the problems constant or only occur now and then?

- Does the severity of the condition vary greatly at various times?

- Did the problem come on all at once? Or was there a period over which it developed gradually, perhaps even almost imperceptibly?

- What does the tinnitus sound like? Is it high-pitched, low-pitched or just a vague noise without any apparent specific pitch?

- Have you ever experienced vertigo (dizziness)? If so, do you suffer from it all the time, frequently, or only occasionally? How severe is the dizziness? Does it merely make you feel somewhat unstable or does it actually lead to loss of balance?

Depending upon his tentative conclusions so far, the consultant may go on to a further list of questions, these possibly including:

- Have you yourself noted any events which seem to make the problem worse or better?

- To what extent is the problem affecting you other than just physically? Does its existence make you anxious or depressed? If so, how severe is the anxiety or depression?

- Do you often have headaches or migraines? Any problems with your eyesight, such as double vision, blurring, loss of peripheral vision? Any difficulties in controlling your limbs? Do you have numbness or reduced sensation in any part of your body? Have you had any difficulties with your speech? Do you have lapses of memory?

In most cases, the consultant will by now have a pretty good idea of the likely cause of the problem. But almost invariably, no opinion will be offered at this time, and he will proceed directly to the next stage.

The Physical Examination

Depending on the circumstances, this may be divided into three areas: an examination of aspects of your body that aren't obviously thought as being linked to hearing difficulties; an examination of the ears; and some simple tests to determine how well your hearing is working.

While tinnitus may be the specific reason why you've been referred to a consultant, the examination will nevertheless cover all aspects of your hearing. The reason for this is simple: tinnitus is frequently accompanied by deteriorating hearing or partial deafness, the impairment, however, being so slight or its onset so gradual that the patient hasn't noticed it. But, the existence or non-existence of partial deafness will provide strong evidence as to the likely cause of the tinnitus, many forms of which can improve dramatically once any underlying deafness has been treated.

If the consultant thinks that your hearing problem may be a symptom of some other disease, he will look for signs that might confirm the presence of another disorder. For example, should he think your tinnitus stems from hypertension, he will check your blood pressure.

In the absence of the likelihood of another underlying problem, the consultant will proceed directly to a visual examination of the ear, this naturally being limited to the outer ear. Once again, how he does this may vary, but generally this is what will happen:

- The consultant will usually begin by looking carefully at each auricle (the pinna or that part of the outer ear that lies outside the head), pressing and probing gently for signs of inflammation, discharge, or undue tenderness.

- He will then inspect your ear canals, almost certainly using an *auriscope* (also known as an *otoscope*), a handheld device that includes a funnel (the speculum) which is introduced into the ear auricles (the pinnae), then inspect your ear canals, using a battery-powered source of light, and an array of lenses which provide a clear view of the inside of the outer ear. Alternatively, the visual inspection may be carried out with the aid of a miscroscope. Either way, the consultant will be looking for evidence of excessive wax, inflammation or discharge, as well as anything indicating damage to the eardrum or ear canal.

- Finally, he will check whether your Eustachian tubes are opening and closing properly, by asking you to blow your nose while keeping your nostrils shut. An action that should cause the Eustachian tube leading from the pharynx to the middle ear to admit air from the outside, proof of this happening being provided by the eardrum bulging slightly; and then asking you to swallow, this allowing the escape of air from the middle ear and being marked by the disappearance of the bulging in the eardrum.

Once the visual examination is completed, the next thing will almost certainly be a series of simple hearing tests. Just what these may consist of can vary greatly, some consultants choosing to carry out a whole battery of tests themselves, while others limit themselves to the very basic ones, letting trained technicians carry out any further tests that may be required. Most commonly, at least the following test will be done at this time:

- A tuning-fork – a device resembling an elongated fork but with only two tines and of much more solid construction, and which emits a note when its handle is struck – will be sounded and placed near your ears and also on the mastoid bone, this being the lower part of the temporal bone of the skull. As the fork is placed in different places, you will be asked several questions: do you hear the sound? Is it heard equally by both ears? Do you hear the sound better when the fork is near your ears or in contact with the mastoid bone? As the sound from the fork loses intensity, at what stage do you stop hearing it? From your answers, your consultant will be able to deduce several important facts about your hearing, including whether your problem falls into the *conductive* category, that is its source is in the ear canal, eardrum, or middle ear, or *sensorineural,* its cause lying in the inner ear or the nerves that carry the impulses from the cochlea to the brain.

After the Examination

Once he has completed his examination, your consultant is quite likely to have a few more questions to ask. Usually, these will be aimed mainly at confirming his findings; occasionally, he may ask you to explain in greater detail some of the things you touched upon briefly during the first stage of the consultation.

In most cases, you will then be offered a diagnosis, although that may be reserved until further tests have been completed.

Audiometry

Although any form of checking someone's hearing could be called *audiometry*, this word is usually reserved to describe tests involving the use of electrical apparatus.

Modern day audiometers can test hearing in great and comprehensive detail. While checking someone's hearing with a tuning-fork can provide a good deal of valuable information very rapidly, the results are nevertheless pretty broad and will not exactly identify in what range the hearing may be failing and the severity of the failure. While discovering that a patient has a measure of deafness is an important finding, the exact extent of the impairment needs to be ascertained before remedial action can be properly planned.

As you'll recall from a previous chapter, the range of frequencies used by human speech is only a comparatively narrow band of the frequencies that someone with perfect hearing can perceive. While it may be desirable to hear as wide a range of frequencies as possible, the fact is that hearing will be generally considered as adequate for most purposes, providing it is sufficiently sensitive within those frequencies covered by speech. There is also another very practical reason why this band of frequencies is the one most taken into account: most hearing-aids are designed in such a way that they will only bring substantial improvement within that range. What this means is that while the loss of hearing in other frequencies may be indicative of the nature of the problem, the testing of hearing will generally concentrate on those frequencies lying between 250 and 8,000 Hz, with an even narrower range than that only being checked sometimes.

Hearing is tested with an audiometer, an instrument capable of synthetising different tones at varying frequencies at various levels of intensity, the sound – usually a pure tone somewhat like a continuous toneless whistle – being delivered to the patient through close-fitting earphones that exclude ambient noise, or possibly through loudspeakers.

Two different but interconnected aspects of the hearing are measured during testing – what frequencies can be heard and how loud the sound has to be at different frequencies before it becomes audible, the results being plotted on two graphs (one for each ear) called *audiograms*. At the left side of each audiogram there is a descending scale – ranging usually from 130 to –10 dB – against which hearing sensitivity is recorded; at the bottom of the graph there is another scale, this one covering the frequency range from just below 125 to just over 8,000 Hz.

During testing, the technician uses the audiometer to send out tones of varying frequencies and volumes, the patient signalling – usually by pressing a bell button, but possibly verbally – when he detects the incoming sound. Most commonly, the test will begin with tones in the upper middle range – say between about 500 and 4,000 Hz. Typically what happens is the following:

- First to be tested is sensitivity at, say, 500 Hz, a signal at that frequency being transmitted to the patient at various levels of loudness so that the lowest level at which the sound is heard can be identified. Depending upon the technician, this may be done in two different ways: either by gradually reducing the intensity until the sound is no longer heard; or by starting with a volume setting that is so low that the sound will almost certainly be inaudible and then gradually raising the volume until it is heard. Alternatively, a combination of both methods may be used to pinpoint exactly what the patient's threshold of audibility is for a particular pitch.

- The same testing will be repeated for the other frequencies, and the whole thing will then be repeated for the other ear.

What emerges from this test is a clear graphic indication of the hearing in each ear, this being represented on its respective audiogram as a line, its peaks showing where the hearing in a given frequency is good, and its troughs showing where it is deficient.

Audiograms, of course, need expert interpretation, but as a generality, good or acceptable hearing – this being broadly defined as that which will probably not be improved to any great extent by a hearing-aid – will be indicated by the following:

- Sounds in the frequencies ranging from 125 to 3,000 Hz should have been heard when their loudness was 20 dB or less. Most commonly, however, these will have been perceived at 10 dB or even less.

- It is generally accepted that sounds above 3,000 Hz will usually need to be louder than 10 dB before they are heard, there usually being a fairly steep drop-off in sensitivity in the higher pitches. The extent to which the drop-off in the higher frequencies will be considered as 'normal' will be partly based upon the subject's age.

Some of the other factors that will be taken into acccount when interpreting the audiograms:

- The age of the subject. Some loss of hearing - not necessarily limited only to the high frequencies - being part and parcel of the way the natural ageing process affects most of us.

- If some of the readings for the high middle frequencies fall into the 20 dB plus range, then how many of them do so? For example, merely to find that *one* ear provides less than fully adequate hearing at only *one* frequency is usually not all that significant, and does not in itself suggest that the patient would receive great help from a hearing-aid. If the same defect is markedly noted in a group of adjoining frequencies, then a hearing-aid is more likely to help.

Incidentally, it needs to be pointed out that audiograms use '0' as indicating the threshold of hearing, this threshold being based upon a standard obtained by studying the hearing of a large number of young people with totally healthy hearing. Despite that, the threshold mark remains an arbitrary one, with many people whose hearing is perfectly fine for everyday purposes failing to hear *any* frequencies at such a low level, requiring the sound to often be at least 5 or 10 or even more decibels louder. There are some people whose hearing is so very sensitive that they can detect some frequencies at lower intensities than 0 dB, that being the reason why the standard audiogram starts at −10 dB so that these very rare occurences can be recorded without the line going off the chart.

Additional Tests

In most cases, a standard audiometer test will be enough to provide all the necessary data to enable a diagnosis, but occasionally, a *bone conduction test* will also be requested. This is essentially similar to the test described above, except that the sounds generated by the audiometer will not be transmitted to the subject's ears through earphones, but will instead be sent to the mastoid bone through a small device clamped against it. Within the device, sound vibrations created by a miniature loudspeaker connected to the audiometer are translated into mechanical vibrations, these being applied directly to the bone via a tiny piston. Bone, of course, is an excellent transmitter of vibrations, and those produced by the piston will be received by the cochlea (both of them, in fact, although the one nearest to the piston will perceive the vibrations much more clearly than the other).

As this system of transmitting sound vibrations bypasses both the outer and middle ear, tests carried out this way will pinpoint exactly what sounds can be heard by the cochleae and/or transmitted via the hearing nerves. Much valuable information about the source of the problem can be gained by comparing audiograms obtained in the usual manner with those resulting from bone conduction testing.

Additionally, there are many other kinds of tests which can be done should the circumstances warrant it, the main ones including investigations to determine, amongst other things: how easily and smoothly the eardrum and the ossicles respond to vibrations; the air pressure in the middle ears, this providing information about whether the Eustachian tubes are working properly; and how well the *stapedial reflex* is working, this being the automatic reflex that helps protect hearing against very loud sounds in excess of 80 dB by tensing a small muscle linked to the third ossicle, and so reducing the intensity of the sound conducted further along the line to the cochlea.

The Diagnosis

When all the tests have been completed, your consultant will be in a position to make his diagnosis. At that time, there will be two main possibilities:

1) The tinnitus appears to be due to, or is a symptom of, some other underlying problem which can be cured or helped by medical treatment, such as inflammation, otosclerosis, thyroid problems, or Meniere's disease. Naturally, in that case, the relevant medical treatment will be offered with the hope that as well as clearing up the underlying disorder it will also cure or reduce the tinnitus. A medically treatable condition will, however, generally only be found in about five per cent of the cases.

2) As happens in about 95 per cent of instances of tinnitus, the examination and tests will have failed to reveal any medically treatable cause for the disorder, other than, as is usually the case, the disorder is also accompanied by hearing that is failing somewhat.

Depending upon your point of view, the fact that medical investigation usually fails to find a medically treatable cause in about 19 out of every 20 cases of tinnitus, can be seen as either good or bad news. To look first on the bright side, this means that most instances of tinnitus are not the result of another disease whose eventual consequences may be more dire. The bad news, of course, is that most cases of tinnitus are not going to be cured by medical treatment. This latter sentence, however, must not be interpreted as meaning that medically untreatable tinnitus cannot be treated, even possibly 'cured' to the extent that its effects are no longer noticeable, just that the help for the condition will not come in a form that can be provided by medication or surgery.

Drug Treatments for Tinnitus

Just what non-medical help is available to ease tinnitus will be covered in depth in the next few chapters. However, before going on to these, a brief look at some medical treatments, excluding those for specific conditions covered in the previous chapter, that have had varying degrees of success in making tinnitus more bearable. It needs to be noted that only seldom are drugs prescribed for tinnitus alone, and that many of those mentioned hereafter have only been used in trials, the results obtained not always having been fully confirmed by further studies. It's also worth noting that the British National Formulary, a regularly updated joint publication of the British Medical Association and the Royal Pharmaceutical Society of Great Britain, that lists all drugs in common use together with suggestions as to when and how they should be prescribed, doesn't even mention tinnitus as such in its index, although the condition is referred to in connection with other disorders.

- Barbiturates, such as Amytal, are normally mainly used as sedatives, to counteract insomnia, and to reduce anxiety, but have also proven of value in relieving tinnitus. Despite various studies, it remains less than clear how the beneficial effects are obtained in tinnitus, these being possibly due to either a reduction in stress and anxiety or a lessened perception of tinnitus, or even a combination of both of these factors. Whatever may be the true explanation, barbiturates do work for many tinnitus sufferers. However, there are also lots of good reasons why doctors are usually reluctant to prescribe these drugs. Firstly, patients can quickly become dependent on them; secondly, the beneficial effects may soon decrease as tolerance sets in, the combination of these factors all too often leading to a situation where the drug does little to aid the problem for which it was prescribed in the first place, but is still being prescribed to avoid the problems that may accompany withdrawal. Additionally, the long-term use of barbiturates can lead to severe side-effects, including permanent damage to the liver.

- Several studies have been done on the effect of lignocaine, also known as lidocaine, upon tinnitus. Normally, these drugs are used as local anaesthetics or for regularising erratic heart rhythms, but it was found that injections of lignocaine could bring substantial relief from tinnitus, even clearing it completely in some patients. Unfortunately, the relief is short-lived, most commonly lasting but a few hours. What's more, the drugs can lead to serious side-effects, including confusion and convulsions. Because of this, most experts have concluded that these drugs are not a practical treatment method for tinnitus, although further research continues, much of it concentrating on a form of lignocaine that can be taken orally.

- Tranquillisers - such as diazepam or lorazepam - are quite frequently prescribed for tinnitus sufferers, although it is not believed that these drugs have any effect whatever on the disorder itself, their value being confined to enabling the patient to cope better with the symptoms. Although exact figures are lacking, it is believed that a sizeable number of tinnitus sufferers are receiving regular prescriptions for tranquillisers. Various studies have reported greatly conflicting evidence about the value of such treatment, For example, one research project found that two thirds of tinnitus sufferers were helped by taking a minor tranquilliser, while other studies concluded that the benefits of such a regime were outweighed by the risks of side-effects and possible dependence. It seems that the extent to which tranquillisers can help is very much an individual matter, although such facts as are currently available strongly suggest these drugs are most likely to be of substantial benefit when a) the tinnitus is quite severe, and b) the patient also has other problems related to stress and/or anxiety.

- Tricyclic and related antidepressants are known to often exacerbate tinnitus, but paradoxically may help some sufferers. Once again, it is less than clear just how the drugs provide benefits in tinnitus, but some experts believe that this may be due to an anticonvulsive effect; others, considering the links between stress, anxiety and depression, find a simpler explanation. One intriguing aspect of these antidepressants is that they can help reduce oral and facial pain, this leading some researchers to speculate just how they may also affect the nerves involved in the hearing process.

Summing It Up

The above are, of course, just a few of the drugs that have been tried in tinnitus. Unfortunately, none has to date proven itself sufficiently effective to be described as a treatment of choice. However, this does not mean that drug therapy may not provide valuable relief for many tinnitus sufferers, just that the results are often unpredictable and, that any benefits have to be carefully weighed against the risks of side-effects and dependence that any long-term drug regime usually involves.

In the next chapter, we will look at other ways of reducing the impact of tinnitus, especially by avoiding or reducing our exposure to things that may either trigger it or make it worse.

CHAPTER 7

Reducing the Impact of Tinnitus

While medical treatments are unfortunately only likely to be of great help for a relatively small minority of sufferers from tinnitus, there are many other ways in which the impact of the symptoms can be substantially reduced, even possibly completely eliminated.

These non-medical forms of help fall into three main categories:

1) The identification – and thereafter the avoidance – of those things that may set off the symptoms and/or make them worse.

2) Electronic devices, such as hearing-aids and tinnitus maskers. These reduce the effect of tinnitus either by improving the hearing as a whole or, minimise tinnitus by introducing other sounds that have a tendency to 'cancel' them out. For more details, see the next chapter.

3) Different ways of seeking to alter how strongly the sufferer reacts to tinnitus, this hopefully leading to a lessened perception of the noises and thereby making the disorder more acceptable and less intrusive or disabling. This latter approach, which usually relies on methods to reduce stress and anxiety, is, in fact, closely interwoven with preventing the symptoms from arising in the first place. See Chapters 9 and 10.

In this chapter, we will be concentrating on those things that for many people make tinnitus worse, if not necessarily causing it. However, before we proceed, a note of explanation and caution is in order:

Subjective tinnitus invariably manifests itself in a very individual way with probably no two sufferers experiencing it identically. Equally individualistic are the things that can make the disorder better or worse for a given sufferer. This means that the suggestions and recommendations that follow, although suitable for the vast majority of people with tinnitus, will not always work in every case. For example, while giving up smoking will probably help most sufferers, there are those for whom the stress of nicotine withdrawal may perhaps precipitate worse symptoms than ever before. Readers are therefore strongly urged to consider the following facts in the light of their own individual circumstances.

Food Allergy and Tinnitus

There is little doubt that many instances of tinnitus are worsened by eating certain foods, whether this be due to a side-effect of an allergic reaction to the food or a substance in the food causing a direct effect. Like tinnitus, food allergy is a very individualistic problem, and there are no hard and fast rules that say that this or that food will make tinnitus worse for everyone. Nevertheless, there are some foods that time and time again have been identified by tinnitus sufferers as worsening their symptoms, and it would certainly be worth trying to avoid these for some time to see whether that makes any appreciable difference in your case. Incidentally, also mentioned are foods linked to hearing loss in general, as tinnitus and hearing loss often occur together, and improving hearing often reduces accompanying tinnitus. Foods most likely to be 'offenders' include:

- Coffee, tea, and other drinks – such as colas – that contain caffeine, a powerful stimulant. Although caffeine's initial effect is that of a pick-me-up, the temporary boost this produces is soon followed by a let-down, and researchers have found that this see-sawing between mild highs and lows can heighten anxiety as well as bring on depression in susceptible people. Decaffeinated coffee and tea appear to have no effect on tinnitus.

- A similar effect to that of caffeine has been attributed to cocoa, which, of course, is mainly found in chocolate, pastries, cakes, and chocolate drinks, but it is also often one of the ingredients of processed and/or packaged foods.

- Foods high in saturated fats have also been implicated, these, of course, being likely to raise your cholesterol level, so possibly leading to hypertension, a condition strongly associated with tinnitus. Additionally, several studies have confirmed a link between sensorineural hearing loss and high levels of blood fats. This probably being due to high blood fat levels causing hearing loss by restricting the supply of oxygen and nutrients to the inner ear. Further research has shown that following a diet that's low in saturated fats provides some protection against hearing loss, and can even help bring improvement for those who have already lost some hearing.

- Alcohol. The evidence about the adverse effect of alcohol in tinnitus is rather mixed: generally, most studies have found that for most sufferers, alcoholic beverages tend to make the condition worse, but some patients have reported that alcohol improved matters for them. It's worth noting that alcohol, seen by many people as a stimulant, is in fact a sedative, and that may account why it may be beneficial in small amounts for patients whose tinnitus is strongly linked to stress. Naturally, should you find that the odd drink now and then helps you, then there would be little point in giving up alcohol, unless there were other good reasons for doing so. Do, however, keep your consumption to a safe level, this having been defined as up to 21 units a week for men and 14 for women. A unit being a half pint of beer, a pub measure of spirits, or a standard glass of wine.

- Cutting down your salt intake may reduce your tinnitus, according to many sufferers. Apart from being more sparing with the salt, remember that many processed foods also have a high salt content, and you should seek to avoid these.

- A high intake of sugar, say researchers, can be instrumental in bringing about hearing loss. Scientists believe that this happens because sugar stimulates the release of adrenalin, and this can reduce the oxygenated blood supply to the inner ear by constricting the very small arteries that supply it. Improvements in hearing, as well as occasionally reduced tinnitus, have been reported by some sufferers when they reduced their intake of sugar and other refined carbohydrates.

- Food allergy in general has been strongly linked to frequent bouts of middle ear inflammation, a disorder which, if left untreated, can eventually cause damage to the ossicles. In one major study involving more than a hundred subjects with frequent or chronic ear infections, it was found that more than three quarters of them were allergic to one or more common foods. When the implicated foods were withdrawn from their diets, three out of four of the subjects had either no further ear infections or only experiencing them very occasionally. The most common foods creating an allergic reaction were milk, eggs, wheat products, peanuts and soya bean products.

The specific foods mentioned above are those which have often been implicated in tinnitus. However, judging from patients' own accounts, just about any food may be a source of trouble, there often being no logical explanation as to why eating a given food should exacerbate tinnitus.

If you suspect some of the foods you eat are making your symptoms worse, begin by eliminating a few of the ones listed above for a week or two. If that makes, no difference, then eliminate another lot for a while, continuing in this manner until at one time or another you've eliminated all of these. Should none of this help, then you can try keeping a diary in which you note both the foods you eat and record the severity of your tinnitus. Do this for a couple of weeks and then look back on your entries, analysing and comparing them. If you're lucky, you may almost immediately spot a direct correlation between having eaten a certain food, say eggs, and experiencing worsening symptoms.

However, the link is often not as obvious as the one suggested above, and you need to bear in mind that there could be a substantial period of time separating a 'food' cause and the resultant event. As this time-lag can be as long as three days or even longer, it may require a lot of patient detective work on your part before a pattern reveals itself.

Some Foods That May Help

Several nutritional deficiencies have been associated with some kinds of sensorineural hearing loss and, by extension, with the development of tinnitus. While there is no absolute scientific proof that ensuring that your diet contains an adequate amount of these nutrients will help with either hearing loss and/or tinnitus, it is obviously a sensible thing to do. Remember, however, that if you seek to make up a shortfall of any nutrient by taking supplements, you should first of all consult your doctor.

Associated with hearing loss are deficiencies of:

- Vitamin A (Retinol). Good natural sources of this vitamin include fresh vegetables (especially those that are green or yellow), cod-liver oil, liver, milk and butter.

- Vitamin D (Cholecalciferol). Good natural sources of this vitamin include cod-liver oil, egg yolk, margarine and cream. Vitamin D is also produced by synthesis within the skin when this is exposed to sunlight.

- Iron. Good natural sources of iron include meat, oysters, liver, chicken and turkey. Note, however, that too much iron can be just as harmful as too little, because an overabundance of it can increase the risk of arterial disease and heart attacks.

- Zinc. Good natural sources of zinc include lamb, pork, oysters, herrings, pumpkin seeds, eggs, milk, beans, yeast and brewer's yeast.

Drugs That May Worsen Matters

Both prescribed drugs as well as those contained in preparations available without a prescription can contribute to creating deafness and/or tinnitus, whether temporarily or permanently.

Additionally, many drugs that by themselves would do no harm, can interact with other drugs taken at the same time for other condition, to create a new set of potential side-effects. This possibility is, of course, one more good reason why you should always keep your doctor fully informed about any non-prescribed medication you've obtained yourself.

During one recent international symposium on tinnitus, experts listed more than a hundred drugs whose use had been implicated in either creating or worsening tinnitus, about half of that number having also been found to lead to hearing loss. It, however, needs to be emphasised that most of these drugs only affected the hearing of a very small minority of patients who took them, and that problems with some of the medications only arose when they were taken in much higher dosages than normal. What's more, how someone reacts to a given drug is often a highly individualistic matter, just as food allergy can be, and a side-effect that may affect one patient very badly may leave hundreds of others taking the same medication completely unaffected.

Commonly used drugs that are likely to contribute to tinnitus include:

- Aspirin. This most common of all painkillers is notorious for its ability to create tinnitus, usually of the high-pitched variety, in susceptible subjects. But for this to happen the dosage usually has to be quite high, perhaps several times that recommended for ordinary usage, and the medication taken for some time. While it is not believed that the occasional use of aspirin at a moderate dosage will lead to tinnitus, it is obviously sensible to avoid this particular analgesic if you have hearing problems. Having said that, it also needs to be pointed out that some patients with well-established and quite severe tinnitus have reported that aspirin has *helped* reduce their symptoms.

- Ibuprofen and indomethacin. There is some evidence, sparse but accumulating, that these drugs, commonly used to control mild to moderate pain and inflammation in rheumatic disease and other musculoskeletal disorders, may lead to tinnitus or worsen this when already present.

- Antibiotics. These are medicines that destroy or inhibit the growth of micro-organisms and are commonly used to treat a wide range of conditions arising from bacterial of fungal infection. Although these drugs have literally proven to be lifesavers on countless occasions, they too have been implicated in tinnitus, although there is no accepted scientific explanation as to why this may happen. Nevertheless, the anecdotal evidence from tinnitus sufferers is so great that there is little doubt that antibiotics can trigger tinnitus or make it worse.

- Antidepressants. The role of antidepressants in tinnitus is a curious one. First of all, as has already been indicated, they can form part of the treatment for tinnitus when this is due to, or worsened by, anxiety, stress, and, of course, depression. In fact, there are nowadays many experts who believe that antidepressants are a better overall remedy for some forms of anxiety, including those specifically linked to tinnitus, than tranquillisers. On the other hand, there is plenty of evidence to show that antidepressants can create tinnitus, the condition usually but not always disappearing when the drugs are discontinued. The only way to find out for sure what antidepressants will do in a given case is by trying them if your doctor suggests you should. Naturally, let your doctor know immediately if your symptoms worsen. By the way, should you be on a prescribed course of antidepressants, do not discontinue these without your doctor's prior approval, as serious side-effects can occur during uncontrolled withdrawal.

- Diuretics. Also linked to producing or exacerbating tinnitus are diuretics, drugs that increase the volume of urine produced by promoting the excretion of salts and water from the kidneys. The more potent diuretics are used to reduce salt and water retention in disorders of the heart, kidney, lungs and liver; milder preparations are used to treat high blood pressure as well as reduce intraocular pressure in glaucoma.

- Quinine. Only rarely used nowadays, quinine was once used to treat and prevent malaria, an infectioius disease caused by the presence of a parasitic protozoa in the red blood cells. One of the drug's well-established side-effects was *cinchonism*, a poisoning caused by too high a dosage of quinine (or similar alkaloids) and whose symptoms included ringing noises in the ears, as well as dizziness and poor balance.

- Cannabis. Although not a medicine in this country, it being seen as having no therapeutic value, but certainly a drug, cannabis – also known as marijuana or hashish – is prepared from the Indian hemp plant. Because its use is illegal and therefore largely unrecorded, the evidence linking cannabis to tinnitus is mainly circumstantial. However, there is no doubt that tinnitus-like experiences can be part of cannabis' hallucinatory and euphoric effects, but there is less certainty about whether the tinnitus may become permanent.

Smoking

Experts agree that smoking is likely to worsen existing tinnitus, but there is considerable doubt about whether the habit makes any sizeable contribution to increasing the risk of developing the condition.

Several studies have shown that smokers with moderate to severe subjective tinnitus have often reported an improvement in their symptoms after they had stopped smoking for some time. There is, however, another side to that coin in that some smokers who tried to give up found that the stress caused by this made their tinnitus worse. It is, of course, open to speculation whether their symptoms might have improved had they persevered long enough with their attempt to reach the point where the long-term benefits began to outweigh temporary side-effects.

Naturally, deciding whether or not to quit smoking is a very personal matter, but if you do try and succeed there is every chance that this will improve your tinnitus, as well as bringing the additional bonus of greatly reducing your risk of developing many serious diseases. Incidentally, it needs to be added that non-smoking tinnitus sufferers have often reported that their condition is worsened when they are exposed to other people's smoke.

Reducing the Harmful Impact of Loud Noises

Various ways to protect your hearing by avoiding loud noises were mentioned in Chapter 5, but these recommendations dealt mainly with noises whose loudness was to some degree under your own control. Unfortunately, in today's overcrowded towns and cities, many of us are subjected to noises stemming from seemingly uncontrollable sources. As existing tinnitus is often aggravated by certain noises in the environment, here is a brief summary of what steps you can take to reduce noises that you consider to be a nuisance, bearing in mind that a *reasonable* level of surrounding noise is part and parcel of modern living:

1) If, as is so often the case, your neighbours are the source of the noise(s) – such as playing loud music at all hours of the day – then the first thing to do is to approach them politely, explain the problem, and hope that things quieten down thereafter. Should this approach fail to bring results, your next step is to . . .

2) Contact the Environmental Health Department at your local authority who can take action on your behalf if they believe the noise amounts to a statutory nuisance. Your complaint will generally be investigated by an Environmental Health Officer (EHO) who will normally seek to sort out the matter informally with whoever is creating the nuisance. Should this fail, the local authority can serve a notice on the originator of the noise – or the owner of the premises where it occurs – requiring abatement of the noise. If this demand is ignored, proceedings can be taken in the local magistrates' court (in Scotland, the Sheriff Court) where offenders can be fined up to £2,000 upon conviction, with further fines for every day the offence continues after conviction. Even heftier fines may be imposed in England and Wales if the noise emanates from industrial, trade or business premises.

3) Should the local authority choose not to institute proceedings, you can complain direct to magistrates in England and Wales, or, in Scotland, make a summary application to the Sheriff. These procedures, although meant to provide a simple remedy, can nevertheless quickly become complicated, and you may find that it will be useful to employ a solicitor to represent you.

4) An alternative approach, although also fraught with possible legal pitfalls, is to take civil action against the noise-maker. Civil actions can become very expensive and you should certainly seek legal advice before embarking on this course.

Ideally, you should always seek to avoid recourse to the courts, your chance of success being much greater if your local authority is prepared to act on your behalf. For more detailed information, see the booklet *Bothered by noise? What you can do about it,* published by the Department of the Environment, and obtainable from your local authority, and *Neighbour noise problems – What you can do*, a very informative four-page leaflet obtainable from the National Society for Clean Air and Environmental Protection, 136 North Street, Brighton BN1 1RG.

Summing It Up

Most of the information in this chapter has been aimed at showing how following some simple recommendations can help you reduce the severity of your tinnitus symptoms. For many sufferers, the relief that can be obtained from these self-help suggestions may be enough to make their condition considerably more acceptable. However, there are also other ways of reducing the impact of tinnitus, including 'masking' its noises with other sounds, as we'll discover in the next chapter.

CHAPTER 8

Hearing-Aids and Tinnitus Maskers

As we have seen, deficient hearing and tinnitus often go hand in hand, and one logical step towards possibly alleviating tinnitus is to improve the hearing by using an electronic aid.

While not all people with tinnitus also have hearing loss that can be helped by a hearing-aid, many of them do. In those cases, artificially restoring hearing through an electronic aid may also go a long way toward clearing up the tinnitus or making it less noticeable. Additionally, while tinnitus maskers – more about these later – are available as stand-alone devices, they can also be incorporated in many hearing-aids, and should a hearing-aid be indicated, then there's a lot to be said for having a device that can provide amplification and masking.

We'll first of all look at just what hearing-aids are and when they are likely to be useful.

How Hearing-Aids Work

Put at its simplest a hearing-aid consists of three main parts:

1) A microphone which captures sound, translating its air vibrations into variations in electrical current.

2) An amplifying stage where these variations in electrical current are magnified many times – the degree of amplification being selected by the user through a volume control – to produce an output signal that is considerably greater than the original input received from the microphone.

3) An earphone – this being essentially a miniature loudspeaker – where the amplified electrical variations are once again turned into air vibrations, these being directed via the external ear canal at the eardrum.

Additionally, of course, there will be a small battery that powers the whole system. Although all hearing-aids operate on similar broad principles, there are vast variations in their capabilities and also in the way they are presented – small aids often being worn in the ear or just behind it, and larger ones, which are usually more powerful, having the microphone and amplifier contained in a separate box that's worn on the body with a thin cable leading to the earphone. Alternatively, miniaturised hearing-aids can be contained within the frames of spectacles.

But, no matter, what their configuration may be, hearing-aids all work on the same principle: they amplify ambient sounds, making them loud enough to be picked up by the deficient hearing. Useful though these aids can be, they do have their limitations and, therefore will not always work as well as might be hoped with some kinds of hearing impairment. Here are some of the main factors that will affect just how useful a hearing-aid might be:

- Hearing-aids are most likely to be of considerable help when the hearing loss lies mainly in the frequencies between 100 and 4,000 Hz, as the instruments generally produce little or no amplification outside that band. This range is, however, not as restricted as it appears at first glance because it covers the frequencies used by normal speech, this usually being the sounds that people with impaired hearing most want to be enabled to hear more clearly. Additionally, modern hearing-aids also allow for the selective amplification of specific frequencies within that range, so providing a greater increase in volume to those frequencies where the hearing loss is greatest.

- While modern day electronics can create extreme amplifications, too high an output of volume from a hearing-aid can in fact cause further damage to what hearing is left. For most people, the problem won't arise as a moderate degree of amplification will be sufficient. Generally, hearing-aids are most likely to provide maximum benefit when the loss is such that a gain of up to around 40 decibels is adequate. Should much greater amplification be needed, then there's a danger that this in itself may eventually lead to further hearing loss.

- The greater the amplification needed, the greater the likelihood that the aid itself will become a source of noise. There are two ways in which this can happen: first of all, all amplifiers produce a certain amount of background noise. Usually this noise is so faint that it isn't noticed, but as you turn up the volume so the noise is also increased. What's more, the signal-to-noise ratio may worsen appreciably at high gain levels – 'signal' denoting the sounds you want to hear. Secondly, the louder the output through the earphone, the more likely that some of this may also be picked up by the microphone, resulting in the phenomenon known as feedback. Feedback means that a sound being output is also being fed back to the input, so creating an endless loop of distorted sounds that get louder and louder.

There are two main sources of hearing-aids: a) through the National Health Service, or b) from independent commercial suppliers. While NHS aids were once considered as bulky and unsightly, the newer ones do compare very favourably with those you have to pay for, there often being little, if any, difference in the amount of hearing improvement they can bring. To obtain an NHS hearing-aid, you will have to be referred to an ENT consultant or a hearing clinic at your local hospital, who will then decide whether an aid is indicated in your case.

Alternatively, you made decide to buy an aid privately. In that case, here are a few points to keep in mind:

- Make sure that the supplier is reputable and that the dispenser is authorised to dispense hearing-aids by the Hearing Aid Council, a statutory body charged with regulating the private prescription and fitting of hearing-aids.

- Even when properly prescribed and fitted, hearing-aids don't always work out as well as might be expected. It is wise therefore to try one out before comitting yourself to buy. Most companies will allow a trial period, this unfortunately not always been long enough to truly assess an aid's merits, as it can take several weeks or even longer before you get fully used to it.

- While most people are perfectly satisfied with their hearing-aids, things can and do at times go wrong. Should you feel dissatisfied for any reason, the first thing to do is to contact your supplier as soon as possible. Should this approach not bring acceptable redress, the following may be able to help: *The Society of Hearing Aid Audiologists,* Plas Newydd, Usk, Gwent NP5 1RZ; *The Hearing Aid Industry Association,* 16a The Broadway, London SW19 1RF; or *The Hearing Aid Council,* First Floor, Ashton House, 471 Silbury Boulevard, Central Milton Keynes, Buckinghamshire MK9 2LP.

Hearing-Aids and Tinnitus

Just how much relief from tinnitus may be provided by a hearing-aid varies greatly, but it is expected that some improvement may follow for perhaps up to a quarter or even more of patients whose tinnitus had been accompanied by marked hearing loss.

It's worth pointing out that any improvement in tinnitus won't always be immediately noticeable. As has already been pointed out, it takes some time to get used to a hearing-aid and to learn how to use it for best effect, any tinnitus-reducing benefit perhaps only appearing once you're totally familiar with the hearing-aid.

Tinnitus Maskers

The basic principle of tinnitus masking is a simple one: if you're bothered by a sound but can't eliminate it, then the presence of another sound may counteract or 'camouflage' the first one so that it troubles you less, if at all.

All of us mask sounds – if we didn't, life would be quite intolerable, as our brain would be assailed constantly by a barrage of all kinds of noises, most of which would be of no importance to us, but which nevertheless would have to be recorded and analysed. Were some kind of automatic filtering not applied by the brain to incoming sound data, the sheer magnitude of this information would soon lead to a sensory overload.

However, the brain's ability to discriminate between important sounds and those which aren't, allows us to concentrate upon those that matter while more or less ignoring the rest.

Much of this filtering activity operates automatically, probably the result of countless generations of evolutionary change, but the brain can also adapt quite rapidly for this process to meet specific circumstances. For example, someone living quite near to a railway line may after a while become blissfully unaware of trains roaring by – what's happened is that his brain has learned to pay little or no attention to these sounds, recognising them as being unimportant at the time. While a railway line may be an extreme example of an 'ignored' sound, we all consistently and unconsciously ignore many sounds, such as those made by ventilation and heating systems, traffic noises, noises made by co-workers in an office, and so on.

The brain's sound filtering ability is put to good effect in tinnitus masking, a technique that is based on the artificial creation of an *additional* sound that's aimed at reducing the impact of tinnitus noises. This is how it works:

- The masking device will produce a sound, which although perhaps louder than that of the tinnitus, will be of a kind that the brain finds easier to ignore. Although all kinds of noises can result from tinnitus, the most common ones are fairly high-piched tones, and these are not only often exceptionally unpleasant but also particularly difficult to ignore. On the other hand, for example, a sound like the gentle gurgling of a fountain is a lot easier to ignore and, even when consciously perceived, a great deal more pleasant than tinnitus. In practice, what this means is that when someone is receiving an artificially created sound, they learn to ignore this, so the underlying tinnitus may also no longer be perceived as clearly as before.

The masking principle can be utilised in several ways, the most common ones including:

- **ELECTRONIC DEVICES WORN IN OR BEHIND THE EAR.** Looking essentially like hearing-aids, these devices can also form part of, or be an addition to, a normal hearing-aid, if one is required to help with hearing loss. Depending upon the actual device, the wearer may have a great degree of control in choosing or altering the masking sound, altering its volume and fundamental pitch as well as in what frequencies it will be at its loudest. It may take a while for someone to get the full benefit of a masking device as, firstly, the most effective settings have to be found. While audiometry can provide clues as to what kind of masking sound is most likely to be helpful in a given case, the user may still have to experiment quite a bit thereafter until optimum relief is obtained. However, while the masker may be effective in 'blanking out' the tinnitus noises, the user is, of course, initially very much aware of the masking sound itself. Although this sound will be one that is easier to ignore, it may still be several weeks or longer before that is achieved.

- **RADIOS, RECORD PLAYERS, AND SO ON.** Many tinnitus sufferers have found that merely having a radio or record playing at low volume can be an effective tinnitus masker. Generally, this will work best if the external sounds are fairly monotonous, so-called 'easy listening' music working well for many people. It can also be useful to experiment with the tone controls – or graphic equaliser – of the sound source's amplifier, as selecting settings that heighten one or more frequencies in the treble while cutting down in the bass usually makes for more effective masking. In some cases, the greatest masking effect is produced by turning on a radio but deliberately not tuning it into a station and with the volume turned up quite high. The resultant hissing, crackling sound – which is a mixture of noises at various frequencies – often being an excellent masker.

- **SPECIAL TINNITUS MASKING AUDIO TAPES.** A number of tapes containing sounds designed to work particularly well for a wide cross-section of tinnitus sufferers have been recorded by experts. Details of where to get these tapes can be obtained from both the Royal National Institute for Deaf People and the British Tinnitus Association (see *Sources of Help and Advice* at the end of this book for their addresses).

Apart from these ways of masking tinnitus, you can also experiment yourself with a variety of sounds. Some of the sounds that tinnitus sufferers have reported as working well for *them* as maskers have been quite surprising, including such things as washing-machines and the chirping of cage birds. In fact just about any sound has been credited by one sufferer or another as being of help in their case.

Masking, of course, will not work for everyone, but it will do so to a greater or lesser extent for many. One quick way of establishing whether masking is likely to be of help to you is by trying a very simple test. This is what you do:

- Stand reasonably close to a sink or wash-basin and turn on one of the taps, letting the water run freely.

- As yourself whether the sound of the running water completely obscures your tinnitus? If the water masks

> the tinnitus, then there's every chance that a masker will do the same. Should your tinnitus still remain clearly audible above the sound of the water, then the chances are slim that a masker will make a great deal of difference.

This test, of course, provides only an indication and, even should it suggest that a masker won't help a lot, it's still worth investigating further in case some other sort of masking sound will be more effective.

While masking works by providing a more easily ignored or pleasanter sound than that of tinnitus, another way of minimising the impact of the disorder is by reducing how strongly you react to, or are affected by, the noises you hear. In the next chapter, we will be looking at different ways of doing exactly that.

CHAPTER 9

Psychological Aspects of Tinnitus

While medical treatments, hearing-aids and masking devices, and the avoidance of those things that make the disorder worse can bring major relief in many cases of tinnitus, it still remains a sad fact that after having tried all these remedies, many sufferers will still be having problems severe enough to greatly affect the quality of their life. In these cases, relief may often be found in one or more psychological approaches.

However, it needs to be pointed out at this stage that there is no reason to believe that psychological help of any kind will ever actually reduce tinnitus or make it go away altogether. No, such approaches will leave the physical problem which manifests itself as tinnitus totally unchanged, but what they *can* alter is how much the noises affect you, making it easier for you to ignore them, perhaps even to the point where you don't notice them at all, or only rarely so. The rationale for this way of dealing with tinnitus is quite simple: If you can't make a problem disappear, then the next best thing is to arrange things so that it disturbs you as little as possible.

'Psychology', of course, denotes the science concerned with the behaviour of man (by the way, animals as well, but that isn't relevant in this context). This very broad classification encompasses a large number of different schools of thought, some of these based on what at times appear to be conflicting theories and methods. Just how useful psychological approaches are likely to be in tinnitus will vary considerably from patient to patient, but experts generally agree upon the following key points:

- While not all tinnitus is directly related to stress, anxiety or depression, the extent to which patients will react and be affected by their disorder will often be greatly influenced by their state of mind.

- An undue level of stress for lenthty periods is often the first stepping-stone leading to other psychological difficulties later. Any chronic disorder, especially one whose symptoms can be as difficult to ignore like those of tinnitus, will in itself almost certainly be a source of considerable additional stress.

- While they are separate disorders, there are close links between anxiety and depression, one often being the handmaiden preceding the other. The symptoms of almost any ailment – including tinnitus – will appear to be at their worst when the patient is also in an anxious or depressed state, especially if that causes him or her not to make the fullest possible use of such remedies as are available.

- It is not uncommon for there to be a vicious circle in operation in which the tinnitus creates anxiety or other psychological problems; the heightened anxiety then making the tinnitus seem worse than it is; this in turn leading to yet further and possibly greater anxiety. If this circle can't be broken by reducing the tinnitus, then its overall harmful effect may well be greatly diminished by reducing the anxiety level.

Summing up the above, this means that anything which addresses the problem of undue stress is likely to pay rich dividends in tinnitus in two quite separate ways:

1) The less stressed you feel, the less bothered you're likely to be by whatever level of tinnitus you have. Conversely, the more stressed you are, the greater will be the impact of tinnitus.

2) Because the tinnitus will bother you less when you're not under undue stress, the disorder will itself become a lesser source of stress.

In effect, the two paragraphs directly above describe the operation of what might be called a 'beneficent' circle where improvement feeds upon improvement, and which is the very opposite of a vicious one. Looking at it another way, if you've done all you can to minimise your tinnitus and it's still troubling you greatly, you may yet achieve a substantial reduction in how you perceive it by reducing your stress level.

What Exactly is Stress?

In a medical context, stress is normally defined as any factor that threatens the health of the body or has an adverse effect on its functioning. However, psychologists generally prefer a different definition that states: 'Stress is the non-specific response of the body to any demand.' The key part of this latter definition, of course, is the phrase 'non-specific', in other words, a response that isn't necessary or useful on dealing with the problem at hand. For example, getting agitated about tinnitus isn't going to help you cope any better with its symptoms, yet that is exactly what happens quite often.

There are many different kinds of tests and psychological inventories aimed at determining whether someone is unduly stressed, but these are likely to be rather superfluous in the case of someone afflicted with severe tinnitus. Generally, it can be safely assumed that anyone in that position is subject to a high level of stress, the cumulative effect of this possibly leading to anxiety.

While there are many ways to reduce stress and/or anxiety, the ones used most commonly when tinnitus is the main problem are either drug treatments or relaxation techniques, or, of course, a combination of both these approaches.

Drug Treatments to Relieve Stress

Whether or not you should be prescribed drugs to relieve stress as a way of making it easier for you to cope with tinnitus is, of course, a question for your doctor, but the way you choose to present your problems may well affect their decision. Drugs that may be prescribed in these circumstances include:

- ♦ Benzodiazepines. These drugs – of which *lorazepam* and *diazepam* are probably the best known and most widely prescribed examples – were first introduced more than 30 years ago and are still considered nowadays to be a first line of defence against anxiety symptoms. Although the Committee on Safety of Medicines has recommended that benzodiazepines were to be considered as inappropriate for the treatment of short-term 'mild' anxiety, this recommendation has by no means been fully observed by many family doctors.

  While these drugs can be highly effective, their use does entail a high risk of dependence, and many patients have had great difficulties in coming off them. There are some potential side-effects, including drowsiness, headaches and vertigo.

- ♦ MAOIs. The initials stand for 'monoamine oxidase inhibitors'. Used to treat both anxiety and depression, these drugs are particularly effective in treating high levels of stress that culminate in so-called 'panic attacks'. Great caution, however, needs to be exercised with these medications because they can interact dangerously with some common foods as well as other drugs, and for that reason their use is usually avoided when safer preparations are equally suitable.

- ♦ Antidepressants. Despite their name, these can be more effective in the treatment of anxiety than drugs meant specifically for that purpose, and they also carry a much lower risk of dependency. On the other hand, antidepressants can be slow in producing results and patients may not persevere with them long enough to gain worthwhile benefits. Additionally, these drugs have been known to create as side-effects some of the very symptoms that patients are most concerned about, such as apprehension, insomnia and irritability. Antidepressants have to be used very cautiously in tinnitus because they can in fact make the problem worse.

For additional information about some of these drugs, also see the section headed DRUG TREATMENTS FOR TINNITUS at the end of Chapter 6, and that headed DRUGS THAT MAY WORSEN MATTERS in Chapter 7.

Relaxation Techniques

While drugs may bring quite rapid relief from stress and anxiety, this treatment in a sense merely reduces the symptoms that an emotional overload may create. Useful though that can be to get someone over a bad patch, it is not an ideal long-term solution. On the other hand, relaxation techniques when used properly can be equally effective in combating stress and anxiety, this being accomplished without risk of side-effects or harmful dependence.

There are many different kinds of relaxation methods, but the ones used most commonly to relieve anxiety are all based on the principle that the sought after mental relaxation will come as a by-product of seeking and attaining physical relaxation. This view essentially amounts to saying: 'If the body can be brought to a state of physical relaxation, then the mind, too, will become relaxed, so dissipating stress and tension.' For more sceptical readers, it perhaps needs to be added that the idea of using the body to relax the mind – or vice versa – is one whose validity has been proven beyond doubt by countless experimental studies.

For more information about relaxation techniques:

- Ask your family doctor. Many of the more enlightened practices nowadays operate special classes where relaxation techniques are taught to patients who are likely to benefit from them.

- Alternatively, your doctor may refer you to your local hospital where almost certainly relaxation techniques are taught either on a one-to-one basis or in group sessions.

- Check with your local adult education institute. Many of these run relaxation classes.

- Should none of these approaches yield results, you'll almost certainly find several 'do-it-yourself books' on the subject at your local library.

Other Psychologically-Based Approaches

The following stress-reduction techniques are only likely to be available to patients attending special Tinnitus Clinics attached to the Ear, Nose and Throat Departments of larger hospitals. Generally, only patients with severe tinnitus that is considerably aggravated by stress and/or anxiety will be candidates for these treatments which often form part of a research programme.

- Biofeedback training. This technique works by providing the subject with immediate information about a bodily function that normally operates unconsciously. During a biofeedback training session, the patient is connected to a monitoring instrument that can measure unconscious body activities, such as blood pressure, pulse rate, body temperature, and muscle tension. The monitoring equipment feeds back information about changes in the levels of these activities to the patient, either through flashing lights, a needle moving on a dial, or a tone whose pitch alters. Usually, after some practice, the patient learns how to exercise a degree of conscious control over the unconscious function being monitored. In tinnitus, the technique has been used with some success to reduce muscular tension, so promoting overall relaxation, this in turn leading to lessened perception of the noises. Most commonly, biofeedback is used in conjunction with normal deep relaxation techniques.

- Cognitive-behavioural therapy. Based on the idea that the way we perceive our environment and ourselves influences our emotions and behaviour. Cognitive-behavioural therapy seeks to alter these perceptions into ones that are more positive by changing the way the patient interprets events. For example, someone suffering from anxiety or depression may believe that undesirable events are the result of a failing on his or her part. The therapist will attempt to identify negative attitudes and irrational beliefs, leading the patient to see problems more positively and optimistically, thereby automatically easing anxiety or emotional distress associated with them. If a patient can be brought to see their problem as less troublesome, then it often follows that its symptoms will bother them less.

Psychological approaches also often play a large part in many of the alternative or complementary medicine treatments which are discussed in the next chapter.

CHAPTER 10

Alternative Medicine Treatments for Tinnitus

Because there is often little that conventional medicine can do in many cases of tinnitus, it is not surprising that many sufferers have sought help from practitioners of so-called alternative or complementary therapies. While it is unlikely that these therapies will be able to address the cause of the tinnitus or cure it, it is a fact that they can at times be of great assistance in altering the patient's perception of the problem and so make it easier to bear. Whilst this is not a cure, it can certainly go a long way towards making the situation more acceptable.

By far and large, alternative therapies emphasise a patient's overall well-being instead of concentrating solely on a given ailment. This sort of approach, which normally also uses a wide variety of methods to alleviate mental and/or emotional stress, can work very well for some tinnitus sufferers and pay rich dividends in enhanced quality of life.

While the reasons why someone afflicted by a chronic health problem may seek help from practitioners of alternative forms of medicine are often highly individual, the main ones, according to a recent survey, include:

- ♦ If there is no definite, clear-cut cause for a disorder and its existence may be linked to emotional states, patients may conclude that alternative treatments with their emphasis on the 'whole person' may bring improvements where conventional medicine failed to do so.

- ♦ Many alternative therapies have a good track record in helping people to cope better with all sorts of ongoing health problems, especially those which are chronic or where the severity of the symptoms at any given time is affected by numerous, seemingly unconnected factors.

- ♦ Additionally, alternative therapies – particularly those whose philosophy stresses the power of 'mind over matter' – can help a patient comply with some of the health recommendations suggested by their doctor. For example, smoking has been implicated in worsening, if not necessarily, causing tinnitus. While it is therefore sensible to give up the habit, this is not always such an easy thing to do. The support provided by some alternative therapies can, however, ease the pangs of withdrawal.

The above are all good reasons why someone with tinnitus that failed to respond to 'normal' treatments may want to consider what alternative medicine has to offer. In most instances, it's certainly worth giving it a try because there is plenty of anecdotal evidence that for some tinnitus sufferers, alternative therapies have made a world of difference.

Having said that in favour of alternative medicine, it also needs to be added that is is important to be cautious in choosing a practitioner. While the vast majority of alternative practitioners are highly trained and totally ethical, there is also unfortunately a fringe element whose standards are less than adequate. Because it's not always easy to tell the good from the bad, here are some suggestions that can help you do just that:

- ♦ If you've decided to enlist the help of an alternative practitioner, ensure that you pick one who is a fully accredited member of a professional body whose standing is recognised.

- ♦ Although medical doctors aren't meant to recommend alternative practitioners, you may just find that your own family doctor is prepared to do exactly that, even if you perhaps have to read somewhat between the lines of what they say. Most general practitioners are nowadays much more open-minded about the benefits that alternative therapies can bring, accepting that disciplines like hypnosis or acupuncture can help some people control stress levels.

- Naturally, word-of-mouth recommendations are also extremely useful. Personal endorsements from people whose judgement you respect can be a good guide.

However, no matter how carefully you've chosen your alternative practitioner, it's always a good idea to also consult your doctor beforehand, telling them what you plan to do. Later on, you may also wish to check out with your doctor the safety aspects of any alternative treatments you may be offered.

While there are dozens – if not hundreds – of different alternative therapies to choose from, there are some that, according to reports from patients, are more likely to be helpful in dealing with tinnitus than others. Here are brief details of the main ones that are most likely to deserve consideration:

Homoeopathy

Probably the most generally accepted form of alternative medicine, homoeopathy is a treatment system devised in the late 1700s by Samuel Hahnemann. Homoeopathy is one of the relatively few alternative therapies also used quite frequently by some medically qualified doctors and, under certain circumstances, it can even be available free as part of the National Health Service.

Homoeopathy is based on two essential and intertwined principles: first, that 'like cures like', that is that the cure for an ailment is often found in whatever brought it on in the first instance; and, secondly, that 'less is more', this meaning that small dosages of medication are usually more effective than larger ones. Like many other alternative practitioners, homoeopaths also believe that symptoms are signs produced by the body's own attempts to ward off or cure infection or disease.

Homoeopathic practitioners maintain that the human body has an in-built capability to cope with and recover from most illnesses and, that the healer's primary job is to strengthen the patient's innate ability to heal themself. To aid and stimulate the body's natural mechanisms to accomplish that task, treatment is usually administered as extremely small doses of various medications, these normally being tablets or liquids prepared from natural substances and originating from a wide variety of herbal, animal, mineral, and metallic sources.

Another of the guiding principles of homoeopathy is that of 'Minimal Dose', this meaning that ideally the smallest possible amount of the indicated active ingredient should be prescribed, this in practice leading to remedies supplied in a form that is so diluted that often none of the original healing ingredient can still be detected in the final mixture or solution. Naturally, this has led sceptics to question how a medicine can have a therapeutic effect if there is nothing – or at best, very little – left in it of the original 'healing' substance. Homoeopaths themselves are the first to freely admit that they also don't know why these extremely diluted remedies should have any effect, but point with pride to the vast mountain of clinical evidence that appears to prove beyond doubt that it often does.

Because homoeopathic remedies are so diluted, you don't need a prescription to buy them and you can obtain them across the counter in many pharmacies and health stores. While this theoretically makes it possible for a patient to prescribe their own medication, practitioners point out that it takes a great deal of skill and experience to choose the correct remedy for a given situation, as their diagnostic procedure takes into account not only the nature of the ailment but also the patient as a whole. As a result, different remedies may be prescribed for different forms of the same problem.

For example, if you look up tinnitus (incidentally, that heading is cross-referenced to 'Noises in the head') in *The Prescriber*, a kind of mini-bible that lists the main homoeopathic preparations, you will find that the suggested treatment will depend on a number of factors, these including the nature of the sounds heard, such as buzzing, roaring, hissing, tingling, thundering, and so on; whether the condition is chronic or not; and whether there is also observable deafness. Additionally, the treatment will also need to be matched to other aspects of the patient's health. With so many possible permutations, choosing the right remedy and dosage is obviously something that requires an expert.

You can get more information about homoeopathy from: *The British Homoeopathic Association,* 27a Devonshire Street, London W1N 1RJ; *The Hahnemann Society,* Hahnemann House, 2 Powis Place, Great Ormond Street, London WC1N 3HT; *The Society of Homoeopaths,* 2 Artizan Road, Northampton NN1 4HU.

Acupuncture and Acupressure

One of the most revered of the ancient Oriental medical arts, acupuncture was first widely practised in China more than 2,000 years ago. The therapy works by using fine needles – or other similar objects – to stimulate specific points on the body so as to create changes in other parts of it. One of the aims of this system is to 're-balance' forces to improve health.

Acupuncturists believe in the Chinese philosophy that states there is a basic life force – called *chi* – which is composed of two flows of energy, a negative one known as *yin* and a positive one called *yang*. These energy flows course throughout the body along channels known as *meridians*, and disease and pain, say the practitioners, are the result of an imbalance or an interruption in their normal flow.

Although acupuncture has become one of the better established and widely accepted forms of alternative medicine in the Western world, and has a long record of being effective in treating a wide range of disorders, there is a great deal of doubt about whether it can truly make much of a difference in tinnitus, there being little or no objective evidence to demonstrate this. Despite that, there is no question that there are many tinnitus sufferers who most emphatically believe that acupuncture has helped them, this claim being dismissed by most medical researchers who attribute any perceived improvement to a placebo effect.

Acupressure works broadly on the same principles – and can provide similar benefits – as acupuncture with the essential difference between the two approaches being that the various pressure points on the body are massaged by the practitioner's finger or thumb instead of being stimulated by the introduction of needles.

One big advantage of this method is that it is often possible for patients to be taught how to perform this massage for themselves and so be able to continue their treatment on their own, using it as often as required.

Most acupuncturists also offer acupressure, not because it's necessarily any better but because some people just cannot face the idea of having needles stuck into them.

Because it's absolutely essential that the needles used in acupuncture be sterile, it's always best to consult a fully qualified practitioner. You can get a list of registered acupuncturists by writing to: *The British Medical Acupuncture Society,* Newton House, Lower Whitley, Warrington, Cheshire WA4 4JA.

Hypnosis and Hypnotherapy

Of all the alternative therapies used to minimise the effects of tinnitus, hypnosis and hypnotherapy are some of the most successful. The effects of these approaches, which are used both by doctors and alternative practitioners, are well-documented and have at times given excellent results in treating tinnitus sufferers whose symptoms had failed to respond to other treatments. There is, of course, a great deal of difference between the use of hypnosis by medical doctors or how it may be practised by someone whose qualifications are more doubtful. It is therefore particularly important that you choose your hypnotherapist with great care.

Both hypnosis and hypnotherapy rely essentially on the power of suggestion, whether this suggestion comes from the therapist or from the patient themself. In fact, there is a school of thought that maintains that no one is ever hypnotised by someone else; what invariably happens is that, despite appearances to the contrary, the subject hypnotises themself, the hypnotist merely providing a conduit for this self-hypnosis. Be that as it may, one extremely valuable aspect of hypnosis is that most patients can be successfully taught to hypnotise themselves, and they can then thereafter use the technique on their own whenever needed to further reinforce suggestions received during previous sessions.

A good deal of research has been done into the effectiveness of hypnosis in tinnitus, and although there were some variations in the findings of different studies, the general findings were that for many – perhaps even for most – tinnitus sufferers, hypnosis if administered by a properly trained practitioner could bring worthwhile benefits, the technique being particularly suitable for reducing the effects of tinnitus that was exacerbated by stress or worry. Experts, however, agree that hypnosis will not actually reduce the tinnitus itself, but will make it appear better as the patient's reaction to the noises is modified, making them less aware of the noises or increasing their level of tolerance to them. Both of these aims generally achieved by improving their ability to relax and also respond less forcefully to stress.

Despite the claims of some practitioners, not everyone is a suitable candidate for hypnosis, and there is considerable variation in the degree to which people respond to the technique, some falling almost immediately into a deep trance-like state at the first suggestion while others totally fail to respond. Incidentally, there is no need to be able to attain a deep hypnotic state for hypnosis to work, all that's needed is the lightest of trances. Post-hypnotic suggestions can work extremely well, even if the subject's trance is so minimal that they remained totally unaware that they are or have been in an hypnotic state.

One way of trying out hypnosis at little cost and without risk, is by buying one or more of the self-hypnosis tapes that are commonly advertised in newspapers and magazines. While these tapes can be most useful, they are, of course, usually aimed at creating generally beneficial effects – such as creating relaxation or improving self-confidence – and not geared specifically to tinnitus. However, many of these tapes can be adapted by the user so that the suggestions they contain become directly relevant to the problem. Incidentally, many hypnotists will provide patients with an individualised tape they can use at home.

Just how successful 'taped' hypnosis can be was demonstrated in a study of 32 tinnitus patients, each of whom initially received a one-hour session with a therapist during which post-hypnotic suggestions were implanted and a tape was made, containing suggestions that the tinnitus noises were becoming less troublesome.

For the next month the patients were told to listen to the tape once every day at home. At end of the study, it was found that 22 – or just over two thirds – of the patients reported that they were 'considerably' less troubled by their tinnitus.

Although many hypnotherapists are medically qualified doctors, many others are not, and you have to decide for yourself whether you want your hypnotherapist also to be a doctor, this generally being advisable. On the other hand, a hypnotherapist who isn't medically qualified may be more experienced and perhaps more approachable. If you believe that hypnosis could help you, you should discuss this first with your doctor and, if they agree with your point of view, they may be able to suggest a colleague who practices the technique.

Alternatively, you can get more information from: *The British Society of Hypnotherapists,* 37 Orbain Road, Fulham, London SW6 7JZ; *The International Association of Hypnotherapists,* 1 Lowther Gardens, Bournemouth, Dorset DH8 8NH; *The World Federation of Hypnotherapists,* Belmont Centre, 46 Belmont Road, Ramsgate, Kent CT11 7QG; *The Professional Association of Hypnotherapists,* Natural Therapy Centre, Woodland Road, Blaigowries, Scotland PH10 6LD; *The National Council of Psychotherapists and Hypnotherapists Register,* 46 Oxhey Road, Oxhey, Watford, Herts WD1 4QQ; *British Hypnosis Research,* 8 Paston Place, Brighton, East Sussex BN2 2HA; *The Association of Holistic Hypnotherapists,* 27 Sycamore Close, Feltham, Middlesex TW13 7HN; *The National Register of Hypnotherapists and Psychotherapists,* 12 Cross Street, Nelson, Lancashire BB9 7EN.

Yoga

Yoga is a very ancient discipline originally developed in the Indian subcontinent. There are many different forms of yoga, but these can be divided into two main categories:

1) Physical exercises – mainly involving stretching the limbs, back and neck, as well as emphasising breath control.

2) A meditation discipline that aims to help the subject achieve a state of peace and harmony in the inner self through mental control and relaxation.

Of course, both of these aspects of yoga are meant to work together to bring about a 'healthy mind in a healthy body'. However, the physical exercises can be practised on their own.

Once again, yoga – although often recommended to their patients by specialists – has not been objectively proven to be able to reduce tinnitus. But there is little doubt that it can help create a state of mind in which the reaction to the noises is reduced, the extent of this reduction being at times so great that some patients have claimed that yoga 'cured' their tinnitus.

Yoga also has a proven record as being extremely effective in reducing stress levels, thereby being of likely benefit to many tinnitus sufferers. For those who can spare the considerable time involved in learning them, the meditation techniques, too, have shown that they can help reduce the effects of tinnitus.

While nearly all yoga exercises are considered to be safe for a moderately fit person, there are nevertheless some that create a great deal of strain on the back and abdomen, and as such should be approached with caution and only under the guidance of a competent teacher. Sufferers from glaucoma would also be well-advised to avoid any exercises involving holding an upside down position for any length of time. For these reasons, all but the very simplest of yoga exercises should only be undertaken under proper supervision. It's also a good idea to check beforehand with your doctor whether they think yoga is a good idea in the circumstances of your particular case.

You can get more information from: *The British Wheel of Yoga,* 1 Hamilton Place, Boston Road, Sleaford, Lincolnshire NG34 7ES; or *The Yoga for Health Foundation,* Ickwell Bury, Northill, Biggleswade, Bedfordshire SG18 9EF.

Other Alternative Therapies

The three disciplines described above, although part of 'alternative medicine', are nevertheless so well-established that they are seen as an adjunct to conventional treatment rather than an alternative to it. There are, however, also several other complementary therapies which have been found to be helpful by at least some tinnitus sufferers, although there is little or no creditable research available as proof of their effectiveness. Here, however, are some other alternative therapies you may wish to consider, remembering that the mention of a therapy here is not meant to be interpreted as its endorsement.

NATUROPATHY, also known as 'naturopathic medicine', is is a broadly-based system that combines a wide variety of natural therapeutic and healing techniques under a broad umbrella, and it can perhaps be best described as a mixture of traditional folk wisdom and modern medicine. The main underlying principle of this therapy is that the root-cause of all disease is the accumulation of waste products and toxins in the human body, this accumulation usually being the result of a lifestyle that is 'deficient'.

Like many other alternative practitioners, naturopaths also subscribe to the view that the body has the wisdom and power to heal itself, providing that we enhance rather than interfere with this natural process. As far as treatments are concerned, naturopathy relies heavily on herbal preparations and diet management techniques. Treatments offered by a naturopath may include the following: physiotherapy, this being based on water, ultrasound, heat, or cold, or a combination of these; yoga and breathing exercises; biofeedback techniques; corrective nutrition; as well as some others.

A key aspect of the naturopathic approach is that it relies very heavily upon the practitioner and the patient discussing and agreeing upon what therapies to use. It also normally emphasises the promotion of psychological health and the benefits of stress reduction. Although individual patients' experiences vary, many have said that this is a therapy that has helped them cope better with tinnitus.

You can get more information from: *The General Council and Register of Naturopaths,* Frazer House, 6 Netherhall Gardens, London NW3 5RR; or *The Natural and Therapeutic and Osteopathic Society and Register,* 14 Marford Road, Wheathampstead, Herts AL4 8AS.

HERBALISM, also known as 'herbal medicine', almost certainly the most ancient of all the systems of medicine, uses plants and their products to prevent and treat disease. In this context it needs to be noted that there is a difference between what the word 'herb' means to a botanist – to them, it's any plant that doesn't have woody fibres and no persistent parts above the ground – and to a herbalist, for whom it denotes any plant which is credited with having medicinal value. Accordingly, herbal medicine encompasses the use of any plant as well as any part of it, such as the leaf, stem, seed, root, bark or flower.

Most modern herbalists practice their discipline in keeping with the age-old tradition that decrees that medicines are not just used to treat disease, but also are a way to return the body's balance to its normal state, disease or pain being considered as 'abnormal' states. Naturally, this means that a given disorder may not always be treated by the same herbal preparation. As what's the right treatment in any given case will also depend upon other factors, these including the patient's general health, disposition, and even personality. Despite this highly individualistic approach to diagnosis and treatment, there are many different pharmacopoeias – that is listings of specific remedies linked to conditions – and some of these have origins dating back as many as 6,000 years ago when the Chinese first started classifying and cataloguing herbal cures.

Herbal remedies are formulated in a wide variety of ways, the main ones including teas, potions, juices, extracts, bath additives, salves, lotions, and ointments.

While there is a great deal to be said in favour of herbalism, a note of caution needs to be sounded: many herbal remedies are just as powerful – and therefore also potentially as toxic if not prescribed or administered correctly – as modern day drugs. This naturally means that these preparations must be handled with extreme care as they can otherwise produce all kinds of undesirable or harmful side-effects. It is therefore absolutely essential that herbal remedies be prescribed by, and used under the supervision of, a suitably qualified medical herbalist.

You can get more information from: *The National Institute of Medical Herbalists,* 9 Palace Gate, Exeter, Devon EX1 1JA; *The National School of Herbal Medicine,* Bodle Street Green, Hailsham,

East Sussex BN27 4RJ; or *The General Council and Register of Consultant Herbalists,* Grosvenor House, 40 Seaway, Middleton-on-Sea, West Sussex PO22 7SA.

AROMATHERAPY. Similar, although more restricted than herbalism, aromatherapy uses 'essential oils' derived or extracted from wild or cultivated plants, herbs, fruits, and trees, to restore the body's natural functions and rhythms. The essences are prepared so that they can be used in many different ways, but most commonly as compresses, bath additives, inhalants, or massaging lubricants.

Although there is but little conventional medical research to back up their claims, aromatherapists maintain that their treatments can be useful in controlling tinnitus by reducing anxiety, stress and tension.

Bear in mind, however, that some of the oils used in aromatherapy can in fact be poisonous if used other than in the very smallest quantities, and it is therefore vital that this therapy be only administered by a suitably qualified practitioner.

You can get more information from: *International Federation of Aromatherapists,* Department of Continuing Education, Royal Masonic Hospital, London W6 0TN; *The International Society of Professional Aromatherapists,* 41 Leicester Road, Hinckley, Leicestershire LE10 1LW; *The Tisserand Association of Holistic Aromatherapy,* 65 Church Road, Hove, East Sussex BN3 2BS; or *The Register of Qualified Aromatherapists,* 52 Barrack Lane, Aldwyck, Bognor Regis, West Sussex PO21 7DD.

OSTEOPATHY. This is another alternative therapy that has gained great acceptance from the medical profession as a whole. Because of this level of recognition, it may well be that the best way to locate a good local practitioner might well be to ask your doctor to suggest someone.

Developed in 1874 by Andrew Taylor Still, osteopathy has been found to be very effective in the relief of many stress-induced ailments and, as such, can have a role to play in reducing the reaction to tinnitus in some instances. Based upon the underlying principle that 'structure governs function', osteopathy relies mainly on manipulative techniques that are primarily applied to the back and the neck. Once again, however, a note of caution is in order: it has been found in some instances that spinal manipulation can actually make tinnitus worse. It is therefore vital that you make sure that your osteopath fully understands tinnitus and is aware of what kind of manipulation could lead to problems. Remember that although osteopathy can be helpful, it is also a potentially dangerous form of treatment which – if administered incorrectly by an inexperienced or unqualified practitioner – can end up doing more harm than good. It is therefore essential that you should find a reputable and skilful therapist.

You can get more information from: *The Register of Osteopaths*, 21 Suffolk Street, London SW1Y 4HG; or *College of Osteopaths Practitioners' Association,* 1 Furzehill Road, Borehamwood, Herts WD6 2DG.

Healing and 'Fringe' Therapies

Because the success of alternative therapies often relies greatly upon the link betwen physical and mental well-being – a link whose importance is nowadays fully accepted by conventional modern medicine – it can be extremely difficult to gauge what can or can not possibly be helpful for at least some tinnitus sufferers. Even 'fringe' disciplines, have their staunch supporters who say that these have helped them 'accept' their tinnitus, and that this acceptance has made the condition less disabling. Here are brief details of the two most commonly encountered 'healing therapies':

HEALING. There are many different kinds of so-called 'healing' techniques, these including, amongst many others, faith-healing, laying on of hands, psychic healing, spiritual healing, and energy healing.

Healers have, of course, throughout the ages been given credit for 'curing' or alleviating all sorts of ailments and diseases, including tinnitus. It, however, needs to be added that there is but little objective medical evidence to substantiate most of these claims. Despite that, as mentioned in the section on hypnosis (p. 114), numerous studies have shown how strong the power of suggestion can be, and it must therefore be accepted that merely being told 'you can no longer hear the noises that trouble you' by someone in whom you have faith or whose 'power' you believe in, can indeed bring about a positive reaction, albeit that this effect may all too often be only temporary.

THERAPEUTIC TOUCH. Like many of the healers, practitioners of this therapy use a laying on of hands technique. This approach is, however, not cloaked in mysticism and is free from any belief in supernatural forces, but is instead described as being based on 'human energy transfer in the act of healing' and is intended for use by non-psychics.

In Conclusion

Whether any of the alternative medicines described above are likely to be helpful in your case is very much an individual decision that only you can make. Certainly, several of these alternative therapies have helped many patients to live more comfortably with tinnitus; however, the success rate of others is a good deal more patchy. Perhaps the single most important question is one you should ask yourself: Do you believe that one of these therapies could help you?

APPENDIX

Sources of Help and Advice

You can get further information and advice about many aspects of tinnitus from the following:

THE RNID TINNITUS HELPLINE, phone 0345 090210 (both voice and Minicom). Open Mondays to Fridays from 10 a.m. to 3 p.m. Note: calling this number will only cost you the same as a local call, no matter where in the country you're phoning from.

This helpline is operated by the Royal National Institute for Deaf People and they will try to answer any and all enquiries about tinnitus. You can also get information packs and fact-sheets from them, and these are free, although a stamped, self-addressed envelope would be appreciated.

The helpline, which is currently operated by two full-time workers and a team of volunteers, was opened in 1990 and since has handled more than 30,000 calls, or about 25 a day on the average. Says Kathie Price, who manages the project: "The average call lasts about 13 minutes. Of course, there are no 'average' people – and behind this statistic lies a range of enquiries and difficulties. We may receive a quick two-minute call where someone wants an information pack or details of their nearest self-help group. The next call might last an hour and be from someone who really needs to talk things over and let off steam about their life and difficulties."

THE BRITISH TINNITUS ASSOCIATION (BTA), 14-18 West Barr Green, Sheffield S1 2DA (phone: 0114 279 6600). This is the only national charity exclusively devoted to tinnitus, and defines its aims as 'the relief and ultimate cure of permanent head noises'. Its current activities include:

- Supporting local self-help groups, and helping to set these up.
- Providing assistance for research into tinnitus.
- Seeking greater public recognition of the disorder.
- Publishing a quarterly journal - *Quiet* - that provides advice on the relief of tinnitus, and also reports on the latest findings of clinical and scientific research.
- Playing a leading part in the international exchange of information between tinnitus associations in many countries.

Further aims of the BTA are detailed in its *Tinnitus Charter 2000* document in which it calls for, amongst other things:

- Greater funding of the Medical Research Council so that tinnitus research can be extended.
- The creation of more specialist tinnitus clinics in hospitals.
- Greater acceptance of severe tinnitus as a handicap, where this can affect the granting of various Government benefits.
- The free and universal provision through the NHS of ear-worn tinnitus maskers for sufferers whom this would help.

Currently, annual membership of the BTA costs £5 (overseas £8) and this includes a free subscription to their quarterly magazine.

THE ROYAL NATIONAL INSTITUTE FOR DEAF PEOPLE (RNID), 105 Gower Street, London WC1E 6AH (phone: 0171 387 8033; Minicom: 0171 383 3154; fax 0171 388 2346).

The RNID is the largest voluntary organisation in this country representing the needs of deaf, deafened, hard of hearing and deaf-blind people. Its aims include the increasing of public awareness and understanding of deafness and deaf people, and campaigning to remove prejudice and discrimination by raising issues in the Press and in Parliament.

The Institute also provides a wide range of quality services for deaf people and the professionals who work with them, these including information, residential care, communications support, training, specialist telephone services and assisting devices.

The RNID also has a comprehensive stock of books and booklets on tinnitus, and you can get a list of these from them.

Local Tinnitus Self-Help Groups

There are currently almost a hundred of these groups in Britain, and one of them is almost certainly to be relatively close to where you live. Contact either the British Tinnitus Association or the RNID Tinnitus Helpline (see entries above for addresses and telephone numbers) to find out where your nearest group is based.

The activities of groups depend very much on their size, but they generally have regular meetings, quite often with expert guest speakers, and they, of course, provide a forum where sufferers can exchange ideas and compare experiences. Some of the larger groups publish their own newsletters and/or operate a local tinnitus helpline.

The Internet

If you have access to the Internet - the so-called 'information superhighway' - it can provide a great deal of useful information about many aspects of tinnitus.

Particularly worth checking out is the newsgroup 'alt.support.tinnitus'. Accessed through an Internet newsreader programme, this group includes postings from both tinnitus sufferers and professionals. Just what you'll find on a given day will vary considerably, but usually there will be a mix of down-to-earth advice as well as information about the latest research. Naturally, if you have a specific question, you can also post it here and the chances are that you will eventually receive several replies. This is also a good place to make contact with other tinnitus sufferers, this possibly leading to one-to-one contact via eMail or by ordinary post.

For more general information, a fairly large - about 120k or 120,000 words - on-line document about tinnitus can also be downloaded. Called the Tinnitus FAQ (the initials stand for Frequently Asked Questions), it is obtainable from any of the following sites:

* ftp://ftp.cccd.edu/pub/faq/tinnitus.txt
* http://www.cccd.edu/faq/tinnitus.html
* ftp://rtfm.mit.edu/pub/usenet/news.answers/medicine/tinnitus-faq